Editorial Board

NEW YORK, LET OUR DREAMS FLY!

Experiences in the US of 150
University Students from Sichuan Earthquake Areas

Chief Editor: Tu Wentao

Sichuan University Press

特邀编辑:夏　宇
责任编辑:张　晶
责任校对:敬铃凌
封面设计:米茄设计工作室
责任印制:李　平

图书在版编目(CIP)数据

纽约,我心飞扬 = New York,Let Our Dreams Fly!:
英文 / 涂文涛主编. —成都:四川大学出版社,
2010.5
　　ISBN 978-7-5614-4856-4

　　Ⅰ.①纽… 　Ⅱ.①涂… 　Ⅲ.①散文-作品集-中国-
当代-英文 　Ⅳ.①I267

中国版本图书馆 CIP 数据核字（2010）第 085706 号

书名　**New York，Let Our Dreams Fly**！
　　　Experiences in the US of 150
　　　University Students from Sichuan Earthquake Areas

主　　编　Tu Wentao
出　　版　四川大学出版社
地　　址　成都市一环路南一段24号 (610065)
发　　行　四川大学出版社
书　　号　ISBN 978-7-5614-4856-4
印　　刷　郫县犀浦印刷厂
成品尺寸　170 mm×240 mm
印　　张　21.25
字　　数　315 千字
版　　次　2010 年 9 月第 1 版
印　　次　2010 年 9 月第 1 次印刷
定　　价　52.00 元

◆读者邮购本书,请与本社发行科
　联系。电话:85408408/85401670/
　85408023　邮政编码:610065
◆本社图书如有印装质量问题,请
　寄回出版社调换。
◆网址:www. scupress. com. cn

Preface

On May 12, 2008, a devastating earthquake hit Sichuan Province. In late June, the State University of New York offered to accept 150 undergraduates from the universities in Sichuan for one academic year waived of tuition and fees. This proposal drew the attention of the supreme leaders of China, and Premier Wen Jiabao signed the documents.

With the attention of the senior leaders from both countries, under the supervision of the China Scholarship Council (CSC), with the supports and joint efforts by SUNY, the US Consulate General in Chengdu, the Ministry of Education, Sichuan Province provincial government, the CSC, the CSCSE (China Service Center for Scholarly Exchange), other related provincial departments, Consulate-General of the People's Republic of China in New York, and all the universities involved, the Education Department of Sichuan Province surmounted all difficulties with a sense of mission and responsibility, and accomplished all the related work, within one month, including candidate selection, formalities and pre-departure training. On August 15, 2008, all 150 students from thirteen universities in Sichuan arrived at the twenty-two campuses of SUNY, ready to start their new studies and living. This also marked the beginning of educational exchange and cooperation between SUNY and these thirteen universities in Sichuan. Here, I would like to express my sincere gratitude to all those people and my colleagues who have put a lot of efforts into this program.

The students had received painstaking care from US professors and classmates, and they had also been taken good care of by staff from

Consulate-General of the People's Republic of China in New York and the overseas Chinese. Our country leaders had also paid quite a few visits to the representatives. During the past year, the students had learnt a lot from their American professors and classmates, had displayed their diligence and frugality. It is my firm belief that this experience had enhanced their vision and become a priceless part of their lives.

Here I would like to take this opportunity to express my thanks from the bottom of my heart to those American professors, students and overseas Chinese for their thoughtful care of the students, and for their support and help with our rescue work and reconstruction project.

In this May, the students returned to their hometown upon their successful completion of one-year study. We have made efforts to pool the students' thoughts together for this collection. The successful completion of the program has not only further promoted the Sino-US educational exchanges and cooperation, but also made an important step forward in enhancing the friendly relations. This collection will very well prove to the entire world the profound feelings and friendship between the two peoples. I believe that these students will make their best possible efforts to build our hometown and act as the ambassadors of friendship between the two countries.

Tu Wentao

Director-General

the Education Department of Sichuan Province

Contents

University at Albany – SUNY

My One-Year Trip in the States ·································· By Chen Yunxu (3)

A Wonderful Trip to the USA ······························· By Zhang Yifan (11)

The Fleeting Year ··· By Zhang Xiaoli (16)

New York State College of Ceramics at Alfred University

Growing-Up in the Wind and the Snow ························· By Wei Lai (23)

My Childhood Dream ····································· By Li Xiajun (27)

Alfred State College

My American Father Bill ···························· By Lin Zhongdong (33)

SUNY – Binghamton University

An Unexpected Trip to America ························· By Chen Jun (39)

SUNY – The College at Brockport

Similarities and Differences ···························· By Da Fang (45)

SUNY – Buffalo State College

Recollecting the Nine Months ························· By Wei Jun (53)

Study in the US ································· By Xie Li (58)

Those Memories Left Behind ····················· By Zeng Xiutao (64)

My Life in an American University ················ By Chen Ling (68)

University at Buffalo – SUNY

My Footprints in the Past Year ···················· By Ai Ling (75)

SUNY – Canton

Metamorphosis

　　—A Relation of My Nine-Month Study in the United States ················

··· By Zhang Guanghui (83)

SUNY – Clinton Community College

The Clips of My Visit to the United States ················ By Qiang Tao (91)

In Praise of Love ································· By Li Junchen (95)

i

SUNY – Cobleskill

A Year Saturated with Love

　—A Personal Account of My Nine-Month Study in the US ⋯⋯⋯⋯⋯⋯

⋯⋯⋯⋯⋯⋯⋯⋯⋯⋯⋯⋯⋯⋯⋯⋯⋯ By Chen Linglong (101)

My American Teacher Mark ⋯⋯⋯⋯⋯⋯⋯⋯⋯⋯ By Li Jin (108)

Sichuan, We're Coming Back ⋯⋯⋯⋯⋯⋯⋯⋯ By Yuan Yuan (113)

Gratitude and Responsibility ⋯⋯⋯⋯⋯⋯⋯⋯⋯ By Tang Ji (118)

CSC-SUNY 150 Program in My Mind's Eye ⋯⋯⋯⋯ By Zeng Yiming (122)

My Travel to the United States ⋯⋯⋯⋯⋯⋯⋯⋯ By Wang Jiao (126)

A Brief Note of the Journey to the United States ⋯⋯⋯⋯ By Yu Haitao (130)

SUNY – Delhi

Recollections of My Life on an American Campus ⋯⋯⋯⋯⋯ By Jiang Lihui (137)

My Life in the United States ⋯⋯⋯⋯⋯⋯⋯⋯ By Ma Jiehao (143)

SUNY – Farmingdale State College

An Unforgettable Experience ⋯⋯⋯⋯⋯⋯⋯⋯ By Mu Zijian (151)

Do You Have a Yankee Stadium in Your Heart?

　—To Record My Simple but Wonderful Time in the States ⋯⋯⋯⋯⋯⋯⋯

⋯⋯⋯⋯⋯⋯⋯⋯⋯⋯⋯⋯⋯⋯⋯⋯⋯ By Wang Sidi (157)

The Youth Blossoming Abroad ⋯⋯⋯⋯⋯⋯⋯⋯⋯ By Liu Yu (164)

Farmingdale – Long Island – New York – the United States

　—The Valuable Treasure in My Life ⋯⋯⋯⋯⋯ By He Manqiu (170)

A Bud in Blossom ⋯⋯⋯⋯⋯⋯⋯⋯⋯⋯⋯⋯⋯ By Yin Jing (175)

Striving for My Dream with a Grateful Heart ⋯⋯⋯⋯⋯ By Tan Miao (179)

My Life as an International Student in the United States

　—A Year of Harvest ⋯⋯⋯⋯⋯⋯⋯⋯⋯⋯⋯ By Zhang Rui (183)

SUNY – Genesee Community College

"A Touchdown" in the United States ⋯⋯⋯⋯⋯⋯⋯ By Sun Chen (191)

Journey to America ⋯⋯⋯⋯⋯⋯⋯⋯⋯⋯⋯ By Lü Hongjiang (195)

Faramita Flower ⋯⋯⋯⋯⋯⋯⋯⋯⋯⋯⋯⋯⋯ By Wang Dan (201)

Herkimer County Community College

Enjoying Growing Pain ⋯⋯⋯⋯⋯⋯⋯⋯⋯⋯ By Chen Wenbi (209)

My American Dream ⋯⋯⋯⋯⋯⋯⋯⋯⋯⋯⋯ By Yuan Yue (215)

American Dream ⋯⋯⋯⋯⋯⋯⋯⋯⋯⋯⋯ By Qu Mengxi (221)

SUNY – Jamestown Community College

Remembrance of Those Days in America ⋯⋯⋯⋯⋯⋯ By Wang Lei (227)

SUNY – Monroe Community College

Our American Moms ·············· *By Li Xiaodan* (233)

SUNY − Maritime College

Mind to Mind Contact ············ *By Fang Dongsheng* (239)

SUNY − New Paltz

Two Diaries Written in the United States of America ····· *By Tang Xinglin* (245)

SUNY − Oswego

Nine Months in New York ············· *By Jiang Lili* (255)

Facing the Sea with Love and Happiness

　　—For My Short but Unforgettable Stay in the USA ····· *By Tu Meng* (260)

SUNY − Plattsburgh

A True "Flight" ··············· *By He Juan* (267)

A Visit to the USA ··············· *By Zhang Weiwei* (271)

SUNY − Potsdam

The Unforgettable Year ············· *By Wang Yingxue* (279)

Gratitude and Responsibility ············ *By Liu Yisheng* (283)

Stony Brook University

A Travel Experience in America ············ *By Zhang Liang* (289)

My Study in the USA ·············· *By Liu Shan* (293)

On the Year of Study in US ············ *By Zhang Rui* (297)

Nine Months, a New Start ············ *By Yang Xi* (302)

"China 150" Smiles Will Go On ············· (307)

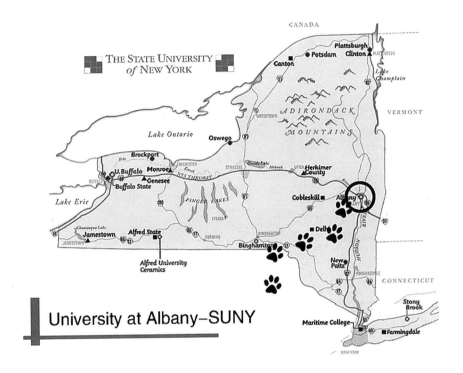

University at Albany–SUNY

(All maps were quoted from http: // www. suny. edu/ Student/ campuses_map. cfm and were revised in view of specific cases.)

My One-Year Trip in the States

By Chen Yunxu
Sichuan Normal University

After a long 20-hour trip, we were overwhelmed by unparalleled happiness, exciting hugs with friends, teachers and family members from whom we had been apart for one year, and rounds and rounds of typical hot spicy Sichuan dishes which we had longed for for a long time.... We have been back to our country for over half a month before we noticed, and everything was just like a dream. My memories come back like tides when I go over the nearly 1,000 pictures on the computer and they take me back to that hot and colorful summer.

A casual try and rounds of strict selecting gave me, an ordinary college student, the great fortune to be a member of a special group— China 150 [1], a member of the 150 students who had experienced the cruelest psychological test but recollected the confidence and dreams toward the future. With the support and effort from many people, we started a marvelous trip to the other side of the earth with both uneasiness and expectation.

Our life began to change at the moment we arrived in the States, and stream of unprecedentedly fresh blood was injected in my life.

Prosperous New York City, serious Washington, D. C., beautiful Boston; majestic Consulate-General of the People's Republic of China in New York and Embassy of the People's Republic of China in the United States of America, busy Manhattan, crowded Chinatown; and of course the well-known Times Square, Wall Street, the Fifth Avenue, Central Park, the Empire State Building, the Statue of Liberty in New York; world-known universities such as Columbia University, Harvard

University, MIT (Massachusetts Institute of Technology) ; as well as various kinds of museums with great collections, such as Metropolitan Museum of Art, American Museum of Natural History... All these that I could only see on TV would be presented in front of us, so real, and touchable. I had been looking forward to the one-year life in the States with great passion and anticipation.

However, the reality was not the same as we had dreamed of. We encountered many unexpected difficulties on the first arrival in the States, ranging from such triviality as the maladjustment of food at the beginning to such cross-cultural communication problems as study problems and culture shock, from homesickness (loneliness because of parting from families [2]) to the adjustment to a totally new environment (getting used to the campus and American social culture), from study headaches caused by language and cultural differences to personal budget management (handling with special scholarship in this program and living expenses [3]), from balancing the abundant social activities with heavy study load (some students even had to balance the time for part-time jobs and studies [4]) .... All in all, various kinds of headaches, which we had not encountered or taken as problems before, popped up. These problems might be the result of our insufficient preparation for overseas study and our limited storage of knowledge. But I would like to appreciate these difficulties, from which we learned to grow up. We communicated with others in our unfluent English, tried to accomplish piles of reading assignments, and had to stay up late writing English papers (such writing assignments seemed to be endless) so as to compete against local students, though we could only end up with a B $^+$ or A $^{-}$ [5] at the beginning. We tried our utmost effort, and sometimes I found myself a machine feeling no exhaustion, trying to take in all kinds of information and knowledge, practicing all sorts of out-put skills. [6] Finally, I got the heartfelt approval from the local people and teachers as well as satisfying as upon my improved spoken English and academic studies. In such a short time of nine months, our improvement in various aspects could not be fully displayed, but the precious experience and courage we have gained are genuine and can not be achieved from textbooks.

So life does not always turn a cold shoulder to us. So long as we keep trying and are determined to learn, she will demonstrate the beautiful side to us.

Unlike the capital cities in many provinces in China, the political centers in the States do not necessarily mean the busiest cities. Albany serves as a good example. The university I visited, University at Albany, locates in the capital city Albany of New York State, so she

Beautiful campus of University at Albany – SUNY

is exactly a political center. However, she is a city of medium size, quiet and elegant, not as busy and crowded as New York City, but rather as graceful as a small town.

People in this city are just like the city itself, lovable, kind and friendly. Actually, as students, we did not have so much time to get to know the local life of campus except on weekends, so most of the good impression came from the teachers, classmates and friends. The person who impressed me most was Danielle Leonard, who cared about our life there. She is the most patient American I have ever seen. She has blond hair and blue eyes, and she is in her thirties. She always showed up whenever we needed help, so she was always the first person who came to our minds when we were in trouble. Though we knew she could not be of help in all cases, we would still like to talk to her, not for support, but for sharing, because she could offer us helpful suggestions like a friend and sister. She sometimes spent her own money helping us out, which was taken as great generosity in the States. We spent a smooth year in the States just because of her help. We owed many thanks to her. The six students in our school made a card together for her before the parting time, which carried our appreciation and best wishes to her as well as pictures with big smiles. On the cover of the card, we also drew the national flags of China and the States with a bridge in between. She was so moved when she got the card that she had tears in her blue eyes. Other people who made our life so wonderful are the teachers and classmates in the East Asian Department: Charles Hartman, James Hargett. Both of them taught the major course China through Western Eyes. They are Chinese culture vultures with great passion and deep understanding about our culture, which made me kind of ashamed of myself and admire them more. Mr. Hartman is a mild person, who looks like Einstein. We nicknamed him "old man." He is good at studying ancient poems (Han Yu is one of his favorite poet in Tang Dynasty) and famous Chinese paintings, and has great interest in master pieces of Daoism and Buddhism. Half of the books on his bookshelf are Chinese books. He was extremely good to us Chinese students with such special experience. He invited us to his place on Thanksgiving, which is a typical family gather-together day in the States, to enjoy turkeys, pumpkin pies with his family and friends. The warmth that night made us feel at home. Though Mr. Hargett is Mr. Hatman's good friend, he is quite different from Mr. Hatman. Mr. Hargett is humorous and likes to make jokes. He sometimes gives students surprises in classes. He enjoys studying Chinese travelling writings and comparing differences between Chinese and Western cultures. He has visited China for several times and each time he spent around one month in China. He was always very excited when talking about Emei Mountain in Sichuan Province, and he would definitely mention his writing about Emei Mountain named *Stairway to Heaven*, and then he would round up his talk with typical Chinese words of humility. The most amazing thing is he speaks better Putonghua than many Chinese do. He really surprised me with his standard and resonant Chinese greeting "Ni Hao" at our first meeting, and since that moment his image as a foreigner was broken in my eyes. For me, he is a Chinese culture vulture with the appearance of an American. I also encountered many funny stories in communicating with

American peers. The most interesting thing was some new experience brought by my name and my special major: I have the letter "Y, " "X, " and "U" in my name, so it is difficult even for some Chinese people to pronounce my name accurately, not to mention Americans who take *Pinyin* as their greatest headache. Whenever I introduced myself to my classmates or friends, it turned out to be a live Chinese teaching class with burbles around. So gradually I gave up telling them my Chinese name, but told them to call me by my English name "Tina. "But still, there were some young American guys determined to pronounce my name correctly. They insisted that I teach them till I said OK about their pronunciation. But the next time they met me, they would still call me Tina, which really amused me. Such kind of fun could also be found in classes. With the popularity of Confucianism and Chinese language learning, an East Asian Department was set up in my school, introducing the languages and cultures of China, Japan, Korea and some other East Asian countries. Naturally Chinese teaching took the lead. I was lucky enough to be one of the teaching assistants of the Chinese class, correcting the assignments and papers of the foreign students who were learning Chinese. We sometimes checked their oral Chinese and did some teaching as well. Not only errors, but also funny usage could be spotted in their homework. Poor handwriting was OK, drop of parts of the characters and inverted phrases were acceptable, but the most "serious" mistake was improperly or even wrongly used expressions. Actually I had a very complex feeling every time I corrected their homework: on one hand, I hoped they made less mistakes to reduce my work and to show their progress; on the other hand, however, I expected to find some interesting new "grammar" forms. For example, the sentence " Oh! My! It is raining again. I am not going"("糟糕！又下雨了,我不去了。") was translated by a student as "My! Oh! Again raining. I am not going again. "("糕糟！雨又,我不去又。") At that moment, I realized how difficult it was to be a teacher and how frustrated a teacher must be when she/he was correcting something so ridiculous. I also realized how our Chinese English sounded to Americans. But soon, I felt it was fortunate to be a Chinese because I found it was never an easy job to master Chinese when I saw the young American guys with blond hair and blue eyes lose their eloquence or even temper and were mad with the Chinese pronunciation and tones. However, these guys with poor Chinese are not foolish; on the contrary, they are extremely intelligent and lovely. At the end of the semester, they wrote, directed, and practiced series of interesting Chinese movies and won loud applauses from the audience. As judges, we enjoyed each of the performances and found it hard to tell which one was the best—all were very good, so we gave all of them a high score. I loved these great guys very much. Though we are at the same age, they are toddlers when learning Chinese, in my eyes. I had a sense of achievement when I helped them master a pronunciation. I do hope they keep learning and their Chinese can be improved day by day. I hope more and more Americans could, some day, study in China as we did in their country.

In fact, there are many other experiences worth recalling: on Mid-Autumn Festival and Spring Festival we got concerns from the university and local Chinese communities; I could never forget the grand event of US Presidential Election, the tree-planting activity at the Governor's Mansion, the figures of NBA basketball stars in games, [7] the live show in Broadway, the special Fountain Day, the episode of the Boston trip, the various kinds of activities given by charity organizations and religious communities, Apple Picking in autumn, ghost-playing on Halloween, helping build houses and backyards for local Americans, making Chinese dishes at host families,

Tasting traditional American food in the host family

cooking the best hotpot with the simplest utensils, chatting and sharing the chores with my roommate Aileen overnight, the lucky socks on which our Chinese names were embroidered given by the American friends on Christmas, planting memorial tree on the memorial day of May 12, happy

Working as volunteers to help local residents build a house in March

faces on the graduation ceremony, touching moments at the farewell party, and so on.

We paid a lot, we sweat a lot, yet we gained a lot, and had a lot of laughter. We also learned to share and appreciate. We got the most genuine care and the most generous help, and to return the love to the society has become the motivation of our studies. My appreciation goes to those who have given me the support and courage in my studies and daily life in this year. Because of you, my boring and lonely life turned out to be colorful; because of you, the ordinary life has become meaningful. I would also like to thank my friends who accompanied me. You gave me the courage and confidence to pursue my dream; you taught me what

Planting trees at New York State Governer's Mansion with First Lady of New York in April

was real friendship. (I have taken you as my brothers and sisters.) Thank you for giving me all the things that could be called precious "treasure," and all these were out of my expectation. I will cherish every bit of them in the bottom of my heart.

Notes:

① This refers to the 150 university students from the earthquake-hit area who were supported by State University of New York.

② Fortunately we got access to internet later, which helped us keep in touch with our families at ease, but because of time difference, sometimes we could not reach our families in emergent cases, such as getting sick.

③ This is a special program. Our scholarships came from different host universities of SUNY, and they were not at the same standard. Due to the high living cost we had to manage our budget wisely to make ends meet and to plan our self-support trips reasonably to avoid overspending or overdrafting.

④ Generally speaking, there are strict regulations upon the time spent on part-time jobs. The limit is no more than twenty hours each week, and students can work full time only on holidays and weekends.

⑤ Grading system of A, B, C, D is adopted in the States to evaluate students' performance. To be more specified, A⁻ or B⁺ might be applied as well. D is usually the passing grade, and A is excellence.

⑥ The assessment of class performance in the States includes quiz, essay, discussion, presentation, and final project.

⑦ Sponsored by the Local Chinese Communities, the 150 of us had a chance to watch NBA games in New Jersey and were fortunate to see the competition between Yao Ming and Yi Jianlian. The majority of the audience was Chinese and the size of the audience was very huge.

Chen Yunxu, from Pengzhou City, Sichuan Province.

I study Chinese Language and Literature at Sichuan Normal University. During my nine months in the US, I went to University at Albany – SUNY.

A Wonderful Trip to the USA

Sichuan University

It was clearly marked May 23, 2009 on the calendar on the wall—the last day of our stay in USA. Looking at all the packed luggage in the room, I finally realized that our trip to the USA was going to end on this very day. Of course we were excited on the day of return, but what we felt more strongly was the unwillingness to depart. I was wearing a T-shirt with several big pink letters of University at Albany, at one corner of the T-shirt the mascot of the university—a small hound seemed to be waving goodbye to me.

On this program, I was allocated to University at Albany—State University of New York. Albany Campus is one of the four biggest campuses of State University of New York, which is located in the capital city Albany of New York State. Here I spent nine special and splendid months. In terms of professional knowledge, English level, independent living ability or life experience, I have gained lots of achievements.

Teaching Chinese as a Second Language, May It Be More Beautiful!

I, a Grade 2006 student majoring in Teaching Chinese as a Second Language at Sichuan University, was given a huge space for learning and pursuing by the United States of America which is the most typical and the most powerful English-speaking country in the world. During these nine months of cultural communication, I profoundly realized the meaning of Teaching Chinese as a Second Language, and I became further aware that it was not a simple matter to teach Chinese. Behind the language is the passionate communication and collision of Chinese and Western cultures, communication between American democratic notions and traditional Chinese Confucius culture. It is this very communication that provides a chance for these two different cultures to integrate and learn from each other. Beside universities, many community colleges offer Chinese courses, too. There the warm-hearted Chinese teachers give lessons to Americans who already have jobs. The experience of being an assistant in Chinese Department in College of East Asian Culture on Albany Campus gave me much more precious experiences. I was very lucky to have the chance to teach in the Chinese class. In the last teaching class, I gave a Chinese lecture on the subject of Chinese festivals, talking about such traditional festivals as Mid-Autumn Festival, Dragon Boat Festival, Spring Festival by means of pictures and stories. When the lecture was over, the warm applauses from the students gave me the greatest encouragement. I felt unprecedentedly proud when I heard them say "Thank you" in Chinese.

Campus Symphony, Cheers for My Own Music

On the 9th of May, on the stage of Albany Art Center, the big curtains were slowly drawn, the lights began to light up gradually, and in the middle of the stage the baton of the conductor Neubert stopped in the air with the last note. The hair of the violin bow still gently vibrating on the string, I slowly laid down the violin and finished my last show at Albany.

This is one musical year in which I reflected the most. Never had I thought that I could join this famous symphony orchestra in the city. As the only Asian, I performed together with the teachers and students of Albany. I loved the musical scores with the pleasant smell of printing ink; I loved the pieces of such masters as Mendelssohn, Strauss, Puccini… I loved the posture of the conductor with the baton, the friendly faces of team members, the big stage, the encouraging look in the eyes of the audience, the program card with my name on it… In this musical world with no national boundaries, all the communications are so fluent and relaxing, so pure, without any impurities. It is just in this process, in this American styled team; that I felt the different performing style of American orchestras. I completely changed from being shy and nervous at the first performance to being at great ease at the last one. The orchestra helped me build up heartfelt confidence and passion towards music. At the very moment when the performance was going to finish, the conductor asked us, again with his usual happy tone: Do you guys enjoy it? Enjoy it, no matter whether there is audience or not. We should learn to cheer for our music, and we should learn to cheer for our life! That's the simplest but most profound life essence I learned from this orchestra.

Apart from playing the violin at the university, I also took violin music to many other places: "Jasmine" at the home of the governor of New York State, "Spring Celebration" at the Chinese Embassy in Washington, "Horse Racing" at the farewell party at Consulate-

With the conductor of Albany symphony orchestra, Neubert

Genaral of the P. R. C. in New York. Even just for a few minutes, each time when Chinese music began to echo, I felt especially proud.

The nine months accompanied by violin music gave me countless cherished beautiful memories. Even if I left the USA with my violin, the lingering sound of the melodious music will still be around in my memory, long reverberating in my mind.

American Confidence Gives Us More Reflections

"This is an interesting question," this is a comment that we often heard in American classes. It's also the most impressive remark to me. Confidence and encouragement are the everlasting themes in the American culture. In class students never hesitate to ask questions. They often put up their hands before asking questions. What's interesting is that, often questions that come across one's mind might be the simplest or even funniest questions which Chinese students may laugh off after hearing them, but American teachers will first give affirmative comments to encourage the students to speak out what they think, to encourage every student to pose questions, even if the questions are silly or funny. But this kind of interaction is likely to result in sparkles out of the collision of different ideas. Actually American confidence can be found not only in the classrooms but also in every aspect of daily life. This kind of ease and confidence can hardly be found in other cultures. Maybe this is a kind of spirit that we should learn.

Unforgettable Nine Months, Grateful and Thankful Hearts

Presenting a farewell speech representing 150 students at the Consulate-General of the P. R. C. in New York

Apart from the colorful campus life, this special team of China 150 has got many special cares in these nine months: the warm reception of uncles and aunts in the Chinese Embassy and Consulate-General, the hot *Jiaozi* on the New Year's Eve, the amiable greeting of Brother Yao Ming, the sincere Chinese faces in the Chinatown, the grateful tears at the commencement... We are such a group of happy kids, far away from home in this foreign country on the other side of the ocean, warmly received and nicely treated everywhere. To quote what I said at the farewell party representing my classmates in the

Consulate-General of the P. R. C. in New York, "Being grateful, we do not need to say thanks. The only thing we can do is to take this warmth we have received back home to China, to pass it on to the quake-hit area, to apply what we have learned to our hometown's reconstruction." Compared with those lovely people who have shown us love and care, compared with those lively moving scenes, words seem to be very pale and weak, but I still wrote down some words by memory, jotting down my American trip as the most shining memory at the end of May, 2009.

Cherished forever—the nine months that let me grow.

Zhang Yifan, from Dujiangyan City, Sichuan Province.

I study Teaching Chinese as a Second Language at Sichuan University. From September 2008 to May 2009, I studied Chinese at University at Albany－SUNY.

The Fleeting Year

By Zhang Xiaoli
Southwest Petroleum University

It was on August 18, 2008 when I first arrived at Albany. The following week was an exciting week, but also the most difficult one in the year. The University at Albany is one of the four biggest campuses of State University of New York. The student population is large, with many international students. To tell the truth, at the very beginning we felt abandoned on this huge campus, cared about by nobody else. We had to feel around for everything by ourselves, such as campus email account, campus card, washing machine, banking account, mobile phone, etc. In those early days, these trivialities could make us girl students cry. But when everything began to be on the track and when everyone was ready for the semester beginning, looking back on those trivial things by which we had been so annoyed, even if they were not worth mentioning, we felt a sense of accomplishment because we made it all on our own. So allow me to regard it as the first independence I gained in my overseas study life.

When everything was on its track, language became a big obstacle. I still remember how excited I was the first time I entered the classroom of a major course, and how frustrated I got when I couldn't understand what the teacher was talking about. (I almost shed tears.) This class completely changed my mood within an hour. The teacher spoke so fast that I couldn't understand those technical terms in English. And the usual group discussions in American classes made me feel that I did not belong to the group. I couldn't interact with the others around me. But the attentive teacher noticed my situation and sent me an email asking why, which moved me a lot. Having learned that I came from the earthquake-hit area of Sichuan, he proposed to offer me help. Thus, my language problem was gradually solved. In American classes, what impressed me most were the activeness and initiatives of American students, and the equal relationship between students and teachers. In China, students are quiet in classes. But here in America, the students say what they want and they pose questions actively. The reason is that the teachers encourage the students to ask questions and answer questions, even if some questions are so simple or the answers of the students are far from being relevant to the question. The teachers treat the students with a kind of encouragement instead of blaming them, which helps them to build up confidence and helps enhance both teaching and learning in the meanwhile.

On happy festivals, one tends to miss family members more than ever. Mid-Autumn Festival was the first Chinese traditional festival that we spent in the USA. The publisher of *People's Daily* (Overseas Edition) in the USA, Uncle Xie Rongzhen, and the uncles of the United Chinese Associations of Eastern America invited us to spend Mid-Autumn Festival in New York. They showed us around New York and took us to eat

moon cakes. The most pleasant thing was that we ate authentic Sichuan dishes at Flushing, the flavors of home food made us not feel so lonely even when we were far away from home on the other side of the ocean.

Cooking hotpot for my host family

In order to know more about American culture, I found myself a host family. The host Eduardo is a jail policeman. This made us wonder whether the jail life in American episode *Prison Break* was the same as the reality. Our curiosity made chubby Eduardo laugh. Then we began to talk about true American jail life. The hostess Yvette is an American Puerto Rican, who became one of the most important friends of mine. We made hotpot together in their house. Even though they can't eat hot and spicy food, when they were faced with this kind of delicious cuisine, they bravely tried it. When I told them that we had hotpot

Working as volunteers to build a house for a number of low-income people at Albany in March, 2009

restaurants in Sichuan, they were as curious as lovely kids.

Whether in China or in USA, we learned to feel grateful when we received so much love. When we heard about an opportunity to build houses for some low-income people, the six of us immediately promised to go. Burying underground fences, cleaning backyard, sawing wood blocks, we and other young and old volunteers were busy inside and outside. When we saw the almost finished house, we felt very happy. Hope that those who live in the house can feel the small efforts that we made and feel as happy as us.

I have heard that people would love their country especially more

The Graduation Ceremony at the East River Park with our adviser Danielle, May 23, 2009

while they are abroad. That's really true. Having learned that Dalai Lama would come to University at Albany to give a speech, the Chinese students union paid great attention and protested against it to relevant departments of the university. Even though I didn't know whether the protesting letter worked, I knew that Dalai

Lama didn't come eventually. The unity and patriotism of our overseas Chinese students were fully demonstrated in this case.

We are not only protectors of our country's image but also spreaders of Chinese culture. Maybe we can't change the views of some Americans towards China, but as long as we tell people a true China, we can play the role of bridge. A small seed can grow into a tall tree. We, the 150 seeds, sowed friendship seeds on this land of USA this year. Next year they will pop up. Next year when our American friends come to China to see us, we'll take on our mission as young messengers and enable more friends to know China, to love Sichuan.

We will never cry again; we just share our tears and joy!

Zhang Xiaoli, from Mianyang City, Sichuan Province.

I study at School of Humanities and Social Sciences in Southwest Petroleum University. From 2008 to 2009, I studied at University at Albany − SUNY.

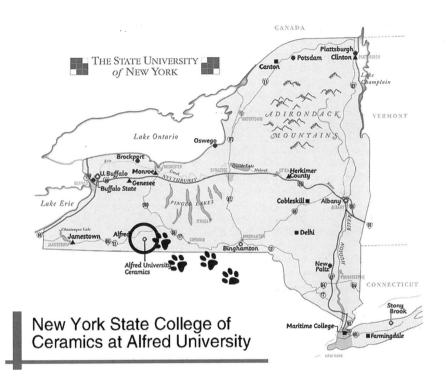

THE STATE UNIVERSITY
of NEW YORK

New York State College of
Ceramics at Alfred University

Growing-Up in the Wind and the Snow

By Wei Lai
Sichuan University

Having gone through these nine months, through tears of farewell, I see the figure of my own standing firmly in the wind and the snow. These nine months, seem to be a real dream. I received the notice about the CSC-SUNY 150 Program in an unusual situation, attended interviews in wonder and fear, and I still felt I was in a dream after I had arrived in New York and seen T-shirts printed with "I Love NY" on sale on the streets. Finally, on a midnight I came to Alfred, feeling exhuasted. I tried my best to drag two big suitcases along the steel steps up the hill and opened the dormitory door in darkness. Facing the unfamiliar vacant room, seeing the moonlight in front of the bed, a fear and uncertainty about the future spread over me. Thus, I began my life in Alfred.

Before the falling of rain or snow, curious exploration fills the life with unknown adventures. I would be amazed at anything different from home on this foreign land, at the very beginning. I was often impressed by the forever blue sky, and by the large patches of

Performing "Heart of Feel Grateful" on the "Alfred to Asia" Show held at Harder Hall of Alfred University

grassland. There were squirrels under each tree and there was shining sunshine behind each cloud. We went to the orchard to pick up ripe apples and grapes; we went to the parks to see lake sceneries. What kept making us feel new was the English language that we were exposed to in each class. When Dr. Pilgram sat on the desk, swinging his long legs, I would look at his tie or T-shirt on which there were always balancing chemical equations or strange but beautiful chemical images. I would also wander between the light sunshine and Dr. Varne's long syllables in pronunciation, and tried to make clear why the inclined triclinic crystal didn't have such luster under my microscope as under his. A moment ago I was amazed at the Frisbee throwing in Physical Education class, then Mrs. Buckwalter's elegance made me feel deeply infatuated in the piano. Gradually, wind and snow showed their figures. When my roommates went to parties and played games, I had to look up words in the thick dictionary and struggled with the test papers called "life is easy" by Dr. Pilgram. The images of SEM (Scanning Electron Microscope) became more and more like man-eating beasts.

In October, the well-known snow arrived. With the sound of snow and wind getting bigger and bigger, I spent more and more time indoors accompanied by books. The first long fascinating dream in the wind and snow was befalling. The five-day Thanksgiving was an important festival, but I was experiencing alone in the dormitory ... all in silence and loneliness. The loneliness was so great that it seemed no sound could pierce through the wind and the snow. The windows became suddenly sound-proof, keeping my expectation, the beeping sounds of warm QQ calls of my families and friends far away. For the first time after coming to USA, I got free from curiosity, busy study and struggling. I was just missing home. After this ice-frozen Thanksgiving, it seemed that I drew myself even up, no longer fearing loneliness.

After all the efforts in the first semester, the winter vacation was long and full of "feasts. " I tried to flee from Alfred; I took a long-distance bus to New York City, all on my own. Taking those seem-to-be endless trips, taking photos with friends, the big rain on Christmas, the New

Year's bell, all these set forward my time clockwork spring—I grew up quickly.

Tree planted to thank those kind-hearted persons

The new semester came, still in the wind and snow. Unfamiliar new words seemed nothing now. Even the cold winter seemed nothing now. I carefully made a mutton soup, driving away the timidity and fears of coldness. Glass Science which I hadn't studied before wasn't so fearful, even the designing of composite material was full of laughter. I felt skillful and comfortable on the back of the horse. I even hoped to get A in the writing class. Gradually I wasn't afraid any more, even in the wind or snow. I walked straight on the snow. I learned to cooperate, to listen, to think, and to make something by myself. I learned to think what I need and to go after what I want. I learned to feel grateful towards others, and to help others.

Nine months seemed to be just a moment. Now it was time to say goodbye. I looked back on the wind and the snow. The wind and the snow were speechless. But I can't find myself of one year ago—curious about everything around, but afraid to touch then by hand. Having gone through all the way, I have gained more than wrinkles on my face, beautiful sceneries in the photos, fluent English. When we left Alfred, we planted a thanksgiving tree with those who had helped us. We hung some hand-made greeting cards on the tree, on which we had written down our thanks, our misses and concerns, and our tomorrow. I wrote my experience in Alfred, jotting down the one year of my youth in the wind and the snow, soaking the one year of my growth in the wind and the snow.

One for all, all for one.

Wei Lai, from Shifang City, Sichuan Province.

I study Polymer Science at Sichuan University. During my nine months in the US, I attended New York State College of Ceramics at Alfred University.

My Childhood Dream

By Li Xiajun
Xihua University

I had dreamt of studying abroad since my childhood when I knew what meant foreign countries and universities. However, that was a mere dream. In the past nineteen years, I had just stayed in China continuing my education. Then, quite out of my expectation, I was granted a chance to study abroad when I was twenty years old. I had never expected that Goddess of Luck would hand me an olive branch on my twentieth birthday.

On May 12, 2008, a sorrowful date for all the Chinese people, an earthquake which registered 8. 0 on the Richter scale hit Wenchuan, Sichuan Province of P. R. China. Hence, parents lost their lovely children and children lost their dear parents. Just because of this disaster, SUNY on the opposite coast of the Ocean gave their hands to the college/university students whose hometowns were hit by the earthquake. They planned to invite 150 such students to study on their campuses for one year. When my teacher told me the news, my childhood dream, that old dream of mine came back to my mind.

On my twentieth birthday, I sat in for the interview organized by the Ministry of Education and my best birthday present was my passing the interview. With my own dream and zest, I began a brand new journey on an exotic land.

I arrived in New York on August 15, 2008. Things passed my eyes like motion pictures: the once distant place was now handy. I was happy to enjoy the novelty and zest this international metropolis had given to me. I was too overjoyed to think of what would happen next to my life.

I took it for granted that everything was going to be fine.

On the 17th of August, I arrived at Alfred University with weariness and a high fever. I was disillusioned by the oldish and hollow dorm room. The sweet scenes of my dream were gone. Perhaps, I had idealized American campus life because I had watched too much Walter Disney campus drama. What was more, I could not understand their English, I was not used to raw vegetables with salad dressings, and I had some trouble in opting for my classes. Worse than that, I began to desperately miss my home, my parents and my friends when the sense of novelty died away. Those hard days raised doubts to my dream: was this something I had really wanted? I did not know. I only knew I had no alternative choice. Since I had chosen this road, I had to go down it. Fortunately, some Chinese students helped us out later. They showed us around the campus and helped us with our option for classes; otherwise, I was not sure how long my haze and frustration would last.

As I was adapting myself to American campus life, my stay in the United States was gradually filled with sunshine. I liked the free classes here, I liked the kind and adorable teachers and friends here, and I liked every nodding and greeting with smiles even from strangers. Each of the smiling glimpses gave me encouragement and bravery. Every day appeared effulgent to me as if the warm sun shined through the blue sky and between white clouds.

Then, I met Mrs. Carla in my host family. This wise lady gave us infinite touching surprises. I was surprised to know about her ten-year devotion to ceramics made in Jingde Town, China. I was touched by so much she had given to us,

Five of us went to Lilac Festival with Carla in May.

ranging from taking us out to restaurants and for short trips to helping us opt for our classes. She led us to plant a tree of thankfulness for the five of us. She took a great care of us like a parent. I still remember that many people were touched to tears by our Chinese sign language performance—"Heart of Feel Grateful" at the "Alfred to Asia" Show. On that very night, Carla wrote a long letter to us, telling us how much she was touched and delighted and giving us her thanks.

Chinese sign language performance—"Heart of Feel Grateful" on the "Alfred to Asia" Show

My dream was coming true bit by bit, and was being happily realized. We left our footprints on this land in the past year and cherished sweet memories that belonged to this side. The visits to the prosperous New York City, the Washington D. C. in rainy season, Buffalo, and the prestigious Cornell University filled us with expectation, happiness and excitement. Those unforgettable memories have lasted up to today and will last for good.

However, time passed so quickly. The seemingly long nine months has flowed away like water. There is no party in the world that will never be over. No matter how reluctant we were, we had to say goodbye to Alfred, to our teachers and friends. After the Graduation Ceremony in New York, we set off, heavy-hearted, on our

The Graduation Ceremony held at East River Park, May 23, 2009

homeward journey. My life has returned to the usual course, but my dream has come true. No matter what we lost or what we gained, fortunately, this is all worth it.

The nine months in America introduced me to a wonderful life and world which I've never had before. It has also taught me how to study independently and live with strong heart.

Li Xiajun, from Zhongjiang County, Sichuan Province.

I study in Material Science and Engineering College of Xihua University. From 2008 to 2009, I studied at New York State College of Ceramics at Alfred University.

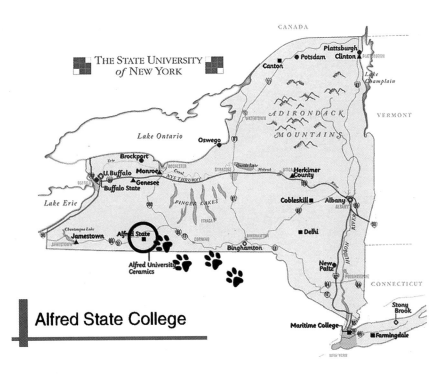

THE STATE UNIVERSITY
of NEW YORK

Alfred State College

My American Father Bill

By Lin Zhongdong
Xihua University

Dedication:
This article is dedicated to my American father, Bill.
I will always miss you, Bill.

"Feelings grow stronger at parting." With the arrival of May, our study in the United States is coming to an end. Looking retrospectively, I have suddenly found there is so much I am reluctant to abandon. And this reluctance grows stronger and stronger when parting is close. I will miss the scenery and even the humblest plants here. I will miss those small animals that frequented the campus. Maybe I will also miss the sharp cries of crows in early mornings...

There are so many people I miss and care about but my emotion toward Bill is rather special. He was a 77-year-old man. I wanted to call him Grandpa but he insisted on being my American father. Bill works in our university canteen. Of course, I knew him when I ate there. Each time he saw Xiaochuan (the only other member of China 150 on the same campus with me) and me, he would greet and talk with us warmly. He always praised us for being truly good and sensible children. He used to amuse us with jokes as well.

As a matter of fact, it was when I got a part-time job in the canteen in my second semester that I got to know Bill. Seeing me come to work on the first day, he was virtually excited, "We guys can work together, huh?" He jollily introduced me to the other workers and told them not to bully me because I was a good girl. Every Thursday when I was in charge of washing up, he would always spend some time helping me to sort out the plates I had just washed and take care of those heavy stewpots. Whenever other workers saw him helping me, they would say to him, "Hi, Bill. Why don't you help me?" He would always answer back merrily, "She is my pretty daughter." It was quite natural for a father to help his daughter. In fact, Bill had retired a long time before. He was working in the university canteen only to kill time.

I was too familiar with Bill's repeated reminders. He told me again and again to call him whenever I felt bored at weekends or whenever I wanted to eat Chinese food. He was always willing to take us out for fun.

At Bill's home

Every week repeated as such. Spoiled as though I was submerged in a pot of honey, I took my well-being for something as natural as breath. I almost failed to recognize that until the arrival of May.

Bill promised to see us before I left for home. That was of course what we wished, too.

The afternoon of May 21 was full of sun-rays and a bit of desolation as well for we would probably be unable to see Bill again after this meeting. He kept his word and came to the porch of our dormitory at four o'clock.

Playing trampoline

He smiled at me and said, "Hi, Claire. I got something for you." And then he drew an envelope out of his pocket and handed it to me. Rejoiced, I took it over and tore it open only to find a picture clipped out of a newspaper. I was in the picture which was taken by a newspaperman nearby on May 12, 2009, when we were planting some trees of thankfulness. All of a sudden, I could not hold back my tears, feeling great warmth surging in my heart. I heard Bill say, "Don't cry. You girls will be back home, will be back to your parents, should be happy." It was true that we were going back to our own home but we were extremely reluctant to part from you. You are our American father! To prevent us from collapsing into tears, Bill said in a hurry, "Now let me give you guys a hug. I will miss you guys." In "Daddy's" warm arms, I gradually calmed down. His gentle kiss on my forehead made me feel as though he were really my daddy, a good father with genuine love for his daughter. How I wished at the moment that time had stopped so that I could stay with him for a longer time!

In spite of our extreme reluctance, parting was inevitable. Having said goodbye, Bill got into his car and waved to us. He told us to hurry back and pack up our baggage, and always remember to be happy.

Watching him driving away, I said to myself, "I will miss you, too." I sincerely wished that Bill were to live with both comfort and self-satisfaction for the rest of his life. Bill, You will be blessed forever!

Before everything else, getting well prepared is the key to success.

Lin Zhongdong, from Pengzhou City, Sichuan Province.

I study at School of Mechanical Design and Manufacturing in Xihua University. In America, I studied at Alfred State College. Through the study, I have come to recognize the importance of being precise. Only then can I achieve success.

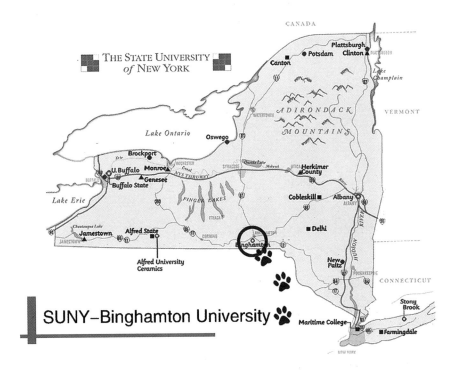

THE STATE UNIVERSITY
of NEW YORK

SUNY–Binghamton University

An Unexpected Trip to America

By Chen Jun
University of Electronic Science and Technology of China

Nine months' overseas life has ended and I have come back to the place where my dream began. Up to now, I still can't believe that I have been abroad. It was really out of my expectation!

All the stories started with that unforeseen big earthquake in Wenchuan. In the middle of July, 2008, after passing two interviews, I became one of the members of the CSC-SUNY 150 Program, which had been drawing attention from different levels and fields of the society. Since then, wherever we went we were being followed by newspaper agencies, TV stations and some other media. In the gleaming flashes, we started our first "exploration" like in a dream. Looking back on these unusual nine months, I find that I have really experienced a lot. From the big earthquake in Sichuan to the financial crisis in America, the shooting incident outside Binghamton University where I was studying, and the widely spread H1N1, I survived luckily. I was really a Lucky Dog.

It was the best season in Binghamton (overseas Chinese students there call it *Bintun*) when we got there. It was in *Bintun* that I saw blue sky, low clouds and green lawns which I had never seen in my twenty years' lifetime. I guess the Heaven of Peace and Happiness described in the writing of a famous ancient Chinese writer, Tao Yuanming, must be something like this.

There are abundant extracurricular activities in American universities. Students like playing sports and they seem to have got passions for sports since childhood. Girls are not exceptional. Here girls would like to be involved in any activity that boys are fond of, which is greatly different from the case in China where girl students would prefer to be silent and graceful. I have got to know a great many girls who like playing football. They are mild in their daily life, but when they are at sports, their intrepidity will never be less than boys'. I got terrified when I first saw a girl knock a boy into air. They play what is popular in America, such as rugby, baseball, basketball as well as football, frisbee, swordplay, beach volleyball and badminton. Surely some American students are keen on playing our "National Ball"—*Ping Pong* (table tennis), though their skill can't be spoken highly of. I could easily beat any one of them though I had just learned some basic skills in my primary school. Later, quite a few American friends asked me to teach them, and with no doubt I became the Ping Pong master in that dormitory building.

On the Lantern Festival party with overseas students at Binghamton University

In my mind, Americans are lovely. Sometimes they are quite serious about small things, which is amusing. I still remember one night not long after I arrived, a bat flew into our bedroom. Having circled the room twice, it stopped in a corner and "fell asleep." It was 1 a. m. and my roommate was already asleep. I was a little excited and told our RA (Residence Assistant) next door about it. To my surprise, he looked very serious and said it was something very dangerous. He immediately called a professional organization for capturing animals, and then asked me and my roommate to get out of the room. We waited outside for at least forty minutes and then came a husky man. He stepped into the room, made an examination, and came out to call somebody else. After about an hour, another strong man finally appeared carrying a huge black box in his hand. How professional! The two men discussed for a while and went into the room. Soon sounds of "Ping!" "Bang!" came from inside the room, and then noises of tables being moved or books falling off the table. After about twenty minutes' struggling, the "Batman" was defeated. It was almost 3 a. m. I really regretted that I should have dealt with that weak and malnourished creature with a slight pat by using a shoe. Such amusing things are not unusual with lovely Americans.

Lastly I have to mention American education. Take Binghamton University which I attended as an example. There are more than 3,000 international students from dozens of countries such as Turkey, India, China and so on. This figure could prove the attractiveness of American universities. They have abundant teaching resources and complete education facilities. Their teachers are elites from different countries. When I entered into the library for the first time, I couldn't believe what jumped into my eyes: the shelves are full of all sorts of Chinese books − *Revolutionary Documents, The General History of China, China Ancient Emperors' Reign Titles and Events,* etc. Even *Readers* are regularly renewed. Computers installed with the most advanced software and application

systems are available everywhere, for free use. The contents of teaching in class are not as specific or rich as what we are usually exposed to in classes back in China. Teachers only talk about key points and give instructions while students have to rely on self-study. Honesty is most stressed in American education. Cheating is something very serious. Even with routine homework, once being found cheating, you are almost "over." Another thing is that there are too many tests in American universities. One of the teachers I got to know gives a quiz in the first five minutes of each of her class. Normally, for every course, there are many

Visiting Harvard University during spring break

home assignments or quizzes, one or two mid-term exams and then final exam. Some courses require projects or presentations. Every process is graded and added to the total. If one wants to get an A, he or she has to work hard and seriously finish each homework. American exams are quite flexible. If the given time is not enough, the teacher will extend the time. If a question is too difficult, the teacher will give you clues. They put more emphasis on enjoying the process than on the final results. They emphasize cooperative spirits. Most of the projects are done within groups of several people. Some courses have group discussion, which is helpful for mutual communication and learning. Therefore, in such an environment, if one wants to learn, he or she can learn a lot.

Later on, I visited many famous universities such as New York University, Columbia University, Harvard University and MIT (Massachusetts Institute of Technology). While I was enjoying the diversity of cultures, I was full of limitless expectations towards the future. America is really a good place for youngsters to strive, to study and to fly with their dreams. Now, I am back again to the place where my dream began. I believe, wherever I am, as long as I have faith, my dream will continue and there will be a day when my dream comes true. I bless myself! I applaud for myself!

Nothing is impossible if you can dream; every dream will come true if you go for it.

Chen Jun, from Mianyang City, Sichuan Province.

I study Micro-Electronics at University of Electronic Science and Technology of China. In America, I studied at Binghamton University. I am a huge fan of sports, which brings me health, passion, and confidence. What I value most in life is my family and friends.

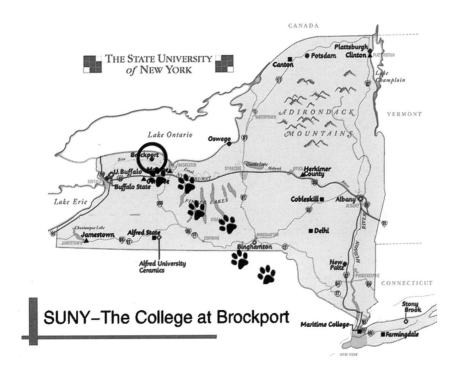

THE STATE UNIVERSITY
of NEW YORK

SUNY–The College at Brockport

Similarities and Differences

By Da Fang
Sichuan Normal University

The differences between Eastern and Western culture have never disappeared with the appearance of the Global Village, but the forming of the Global Village has helped build a bridge between them for better cultural exchanges. This bridge provides cultures in the two hemispheres with more opportunities to communicate with each other, to seek the common while reserving the difference, to promote mutual understanding and to learn from each other.

Cultural exchanges are a process to feel, to learn and to melt those differences. Through the process, we can not only learn a lot in the aspects of development and communication at different levels of material cultures; more importantly, through mutual communication and adaptation, we get better understanding, trust, friendliness and sincerity from deep in our hearts.

The CSC-SUNY 150 Program provided some college students from Wenchuan earthquake-hit area a good opportunity to experience the differences of two cultures.

It was in this period of time that I really experienced the growth and sensation brought by the cultural exchanges. As for growth, it can be regarded as the remarkable progress in acquiring knowledge, independence in living, calmness in mentality, accumulation of experiences in society and the understanding gratitude in our life.

I still remember what happened in the middle of August when I first stepped into this strange world. After the excitement, I felt more worried and nervous. I didn't know how to face a new environment in which the

language is quite different, in which I could hardly solve the problems of surviving on my own. Take "eating" as an example. On the first day, I was absolutely scared when I went to the dining hall. I could name nothing except chicken legs, no more! I also didn't know what parts of the animals the meat came from or what animal meat it was. I had to use gesture language to tell the staff what I wanted by pointing at the next kind of meat or bean food. A strange sorrow attacked me when I thought of my embarrassment at the moment and that when I was at home, I could easily name tens of dishes starting from our classical *Mapo Doufu* to the tiny domestic Rice Noodles with Pickles, even without looking at the menu. I didn't know how to confront this extremely different life. The first day's experience shocked me a lot, which pushed me to learn and stimulated me to work harder and to get to know more people. On the second day, I took a pen and a notebook with me. When I chose food whose name I didn't know, I asked the staff to write the name on my notebook so that later I could look it up in the dictionary and get the right Chinese version for better memorization. Every day I preferred to select different dishes so as to get to know all strange dishes quickly. At first, I really felt ashamed and face-losing to ask for help even with such trivialities as ordering food or spelling words. This was because when I was a child, I was too shy. I used to spend the whole night working out a solution on a math problem, never willing to ask my friends or teachers for the sake of fearing losing face. Nowadays the motivation and pressure stimulated me to study, to experience and to feel all new things with different cultural backgrounds. It was there that I learnt to be modest to learn from others. On the third day when I continued to ask for help in the same way, I got the praises from the staff who told me that they appreciated my behavior of learning new things. This appreciation was a kind of encouragement to me, and it also made me realize the way to survive in the USA. When you are in a new country, when you are surrounded by a new culture, you need to keep learning with patience, modesty and perseverance.

Besides learning from life, I had to handle academic study. In my first History class on the first day, I only clearly knew that the teacher was talking about Columbus, but I had no idea whether the content of the lecture was critical or appraisal, or both. In order to understand the content of that lecture, I gritted my teeth and worked till 3 a. m., reading that thick book of History with the help of a dictionary. Finally I got to understand that by

The square meal

giving evidences the teacher was criticizing some textbooks of History which falsified the fact that Columbus was not the first person who found America. That night I was almost sleepless, for one thing, I stayed up too late and didn't feel sleepy at all; for the other, I suddenly felt the motivation and pressure. The language barrier drove me to spend five, even ten times more energy than American students to finish the assignment or reading. The new contents and the exciting and inspiring teaching stimulated me to study harder. At the very beginning, my study in America is a mixture of fun and pain, but when the semester is coming to the end, there's more fun in study. By then, I enjoyed the real fun in the process of study without feeling tired.

In our life, we are not only in pursuit of the pleasure of study or the freshness of living, but the warmth of real love. I still remember the last weekend before our final exam in December. I went to a party and there I got acquainted with Jessica who then became my best friend. We were lucky to have a lot in common. I was invited to her home for Christmas Week—a real Christmas holiday, a get-together party full of love, a Christmas tree decorated with happiness, red stockings stuffed with gifts, friendliness, smiles, care and understanding. After one busy and warm week of Christmas, I planned to leave for my campus so as not to bother their life, but her parents told me that though I was not their child, they had regarded me as one of their family members. They warmly persuaded me to stay till the end of the winter holiday. That holiday with family warmth has become a wonderful memory I'll never forget in my life. Jessica and I made chicken salad sandwiches together: she minced chicken meat and I prepared salad. We watched movies together. After watching *The Chronicles of Narnia* and *Dodgeball*, she said she liked the legend story of *The Chronicles of Narnia*, and I argued by saying the story was boring; she thought *Dodgeball* was funny, but I said that the hero was not smart enough. We together cheered for her sister's high school basketball match and attended the kindergarten commencement of her niece. We drove thirty minutes to the hairdresser's, singing in the car, chatting about our future and our dream. In this winter

My American family

vacation, we never separated, even a step, like twins. Whenever I recall that special time, it seems as if I were heating up a delicious soup. A small sip of it would make me feel warm from the bottom of my heart. What a memory! It makes me feel warm. I miss you, my American family!

In this one year in USA, I was stimulated with new things, enriched with knowledge and warmed by new friends. In this new cultural circle, I was striving, making efforts, feeling happy and being friendly. I felt the differences, learned from the differences and melted more into the differences. I got knowledge from the differences and I got warmth as well. When I think of the saying " seek common ground while reserving differences, " I suddenly have a better understanding of its meaning. The world peoples have more things in common: the same care, the same efforts and the same dream.

Da Fang, from Shifang City, Sichuan Province.

I major in English at Sichuan Normal University. During my nine months in the US, I studied at SUNY – The College at Brockport.

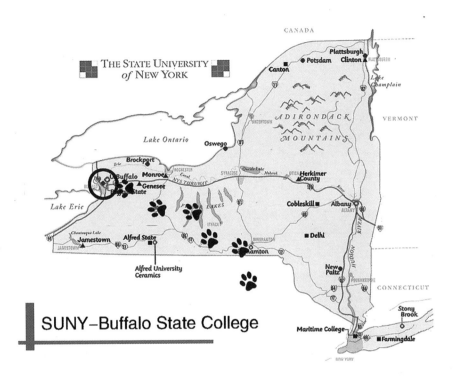

THE STATE UNIVERSITY
of NEW YORK

SUNY–Buffalo State College

Recollecting the Nine Months

By Wei Jun
Sichuan University

It was not until the early morning before the deadline for handing in the essay that I could sit down to ponder over what I had got in the nine months of overseas study. These are nine unusual months in which unusual marks were left deep in my memory.

I turned on the computer and reviewed the photos and began to recollect the unusual experiences in the nine months.

It was in July when I got informed of CSC-SUNY 150 Program. That day after finishing my Anatomy exam, I went home four hours' bus ride away, the first time to go home after the May 12 Earthquake. Around ten in the evening, a friend of mine called me. And this telephone call brought me into the program and my overseas life in the United States.

I was busy preparing for the trip during the whole summer vacation. Then on Aug. 15, 2008 the planes carrying 150 Chinese students landed smoothly at JFK International Airport.

It was in the evening when the flight I took arrived. The project teacher had been waiting at the airport and helped us get the permit of Green Channel at the Customs, providing the best access to the new world. New York showed its warm welcome to us in this way.

The agenda for the second day was quite full. We took the Bus Tour around the city, hearing the names of what we had been familiar with at home, enjoying the beauty and wonder of the Statue of Liberty, the Empire State Building and the relics of the World Trade Center.... A reception lunch was arranged in Chinatown. I was moved by the hospitality of local overseas Chinese. One American Chinese Aunt held my hands and said: "We watched TV every day after the earthquake, every time in tears. Today, you finally came!"

In the evening, the Aunts and Uncles from the Consulate-General of the P. R. C. in New York welcomed us with the teachers from the relative universities of SUNY. We, seventeen students—twelve girls and five boys, were assigned to Buffalo State College. On the third day, the rest of the students flew to their assigned universities in the west of New York, named as Buffalo, Rochester, and some other places.

At the New Year's party in our teacher's house

My general impression of Buffalo State College was that it is clean and tidy, not flaunty. Accomodation had been arranged before we came. I shared a room with another Chinese student, on the second floor. The college also arranged quite a few welcome parties, at which we had Chinese food.

Mr. Song met us in New York and took us to Buffalo. At the very beginning, we were a bit shy and timid. Mr. Song patiently took us to the supermarkets and shops. As we were not quite used to the food, he even brought us instant noodles. When it was very cold, he sent us warm blankets. The warmth and hospitality of our teachers kept coldness away from us.

Festival Celebrations

We held a Mid-Autumn Festival party. I interpreted for a local teacher and explained for her the meaning of the festival. Though my English was poor, she could understand that Mid-Autumn Festival means the family reunion in the Chinese culture. On Thanksgiving, I was invited to an American friend's home. The rich feast of turkey and the hospitality of the hostess seemed to have melted the ice and snow outside. The busiest holidays should be Christmas and Spring Festival. We spent Christmas at Mr. Song's, singing classical karaoke songs. At Spring Festival we took part in the local Chinese Spring Festival Party at which we, seventeen students of CSC-SUNY 150 Program, sang the famous song named " Heart of Feel Grateful. "

At the Mid-Autumn Festival party

We spent Halloween in a local American family. Giving out candies to children, decorating our rooms, we tasted and enjoyed the real American culture and custom.

Days of Snowing

As for the characteristics of Buffalo, snow can be one of the most representative. Located near Lake Erie in high latitude, it's very windy all year round and it is worse when it snows. From Thanksgiving Day to the next April or May, the world covered with heavy snow. We seventeen students who were born and grew up in the south of China only had the idea of the pleasure given by snow; we had hardly ever realized the difficulties of transportation or going out in heavy snow. But our Grandma—Mrs. Blackburn—from the international students' affairs office, had been very thoughtful. One month before the snow season, she took us to the local church for our winter-proof clothes and boots which kept us warmed for the whole winter.

Busy and Regular Study Life

At the beginning I encountered lots of difficulties because of my

incompetence in the English language and inappropriate learning methods. I kept looking up new words in the dictionary and reading the texts aloud again and again, which helped improve my efficiency in listening to lectures.

The differences in education lie in the ratio of students and teachers. One of the courses I took, Recombinant DNA Technology, was taken by only eight students. This proportion makes it possible for the teacher to communicate with each student and we all have the chance to raise questions. In class, the teacher does not talk much, just about key points, inviting the students to imagine. Besides previewing and reviewing, lots of homework is assigned. Students are also required to do research and group discussion, which is good for inspiring thoughts and fostering abilities. Take Microbiology course as example. Last semester, for experiment exam, each of us got a small bottle of culture agent with unknown microbes. We were required to do the test with the methods had learnt in class.

American universities put emphasis on discussion, and each student has the chance to give presentations. In my Medical Anthropology class, the teacher would address the viewpoints of different cultures towards medicine. When talking about our traditional Chinese medicine, he stopped and asked me to try my best to point out his mistakes in aspects like the location of *Dantian*(丹田) and *Renzhong*(人中) in traditional Chinese medicine, the theory of *Yin*(阴) and *Yang*(阳), etc. In fact his knowledge about *Yin* and *Yang*, *Fengshui*(风水) and *Wuxing*(五行) was far beyond my imagination. I admire his rigorous scholarship.

Everyone has his or her own ideas, and is happy to present his or her ideas. And everyone is ready to listen to others' ideas. This is one of the characteristics of American classes that I experienced.

In American universities there are a lot of quizzes and exams. The final exams only account for a small fraction of the final score. American teachers like students to work hard during the course and prepare for each exam seriously instead of being crazy at working for the final exam at the end of the semester.

Universities allow students a long summer vacation so that students can work. Many American students work part-time. An interesting phenomenon is that there are some students whose children go to junior school or high school. A mother student told me that she lost her job because of the financial crisis and now she returned to university for another degree so that she could get a better job. Though no longer young, she worked very hard and got as good grades as others. Students are allowed to eat in class, but not allowed to make phone calls or send text messages or interrupt the teacher without permission. In their words, students respect academics and truth, not simply teachers or authority. I was deeply impressed by this comment.

Farewell

Recalling the nine months in the USA, I feel that time really flies. Nine months passed before I had time to taste it. We lost a little but gained much more. I still remember what one of the teachers told me on the New York coach: "What we should remember and possess is a grateful heart. " I think this is one of the bits I have learned in my study in America. Learn to be grateful, spread the spirit of gratitude, and warm those who are in need of our help.

The most important thing we need to remember is having a grateful heart. Learn to be grateful, spread this spirit, and warm those people who need our help.

Wei Jun, from Jiangyou City, Sichuan Province.

I am now studying at College of Preclinical Medicine and Forensic Medicine, Sichuan University. In America, I studied at SUNY – Buffalo State College.

Study in the US

By Xie Li
Southwest Jiaotong University

On August 15, 2008, with the best wishes and expectations of our family members, teachers and classmates, we set off confidently on a journey to the USA. The year in the US witnessed our experiences, feelings and growth.

Festivals

Celebrating the Mid-Autumn Festival with Ms. Liao from Taiwan

In the US, we could not only celebrate with American friends their festivals like Thanksgiving, Halloween and Christmas, feeling the charm of traditional western festivals, but also intoxicated ourselves in traditional Chinese festivals such as Mid-Autumn Festival and Spring Festival. I could see my American friends' zest for a country with a long civilization. When they were preparing turkey for their Thanksgiving Eve dinner, we were longing for moon cakes for this year's Mid-Autumn Festival. To drive away the feeling of loneliness of us away from home, the Chinese teachers in the university invited us to enjoy the moon cakes and moonlight with them. With the care and help of the local teachers, all the CSC-SUNY 150 Program students in different universities of SUNY had an enjoyable and unforgettable Mid-Autumn Festival. As for the Spring Festival, the most important festival, we also had some grand ceremonies. At Western New York Chinese New Year celebration, seventeen of us from Buffalo Campus directed and performed the song "Heart of Feel Grateful" which won the applause of everyone. Full of gratitude, we waved goodbye to the unusual Year of 2008 and welcomed the lucky and happy Year of the Ox with sincere gratitude to those who have helped us.

Of course, when celebrating our festivals, we were pleased to participate in the celebration of American festivals.

At Halloween, we helped with the decoration of the haunted house and some students were brave enough to play roles of ghost. In the waves of screams, with the fanciful pumpkin lanterns in the streets, in the joyful cry of "Trick or Treat" of some children, we experienced what we had read in

Enjoying Christmas at the house of American teacher Cathy

textbooks.

Thanksgiving and Christmas are the two most important festivals in the US and a time for family reunion, so we were invited to some local families for celebration: some to the families of American teachers, some to host families, and others to the families of Chinese teachers in the US. Anyway, we were enveloped in a holiday atmosphere. Due to the financial crisis, many Christmas trees were made simpler, and even the sale on Christmas Eve could not attract many consumers. These minor changes made us aware of the impact of this global crisis. With the help of so many people, we experienced many interesting western festivals; meanwhile, we also showed the charm of traditional Chinese festivals to those Americans who loved China.

Our Life

Food is a major part of our life. When one comes to a new place, one can experience its culture through the food. American food is "green" but not "green." Their salad is natural food with fresh vegetable leaves, mushroom and salad dressing. We were surprised when we just came to this country and saw people enjoying their raw food. Later on we realized the importance of vitamins after we had taken too much hamburgers and pizzas, and thus we swallowed the raw vegetables.

There is a window serving Chinese food at the university canteen, which we call American-

Making biscuits at host family

style Chinese food. But later on, we found the rice harder and harder, vegetables cooked more and more lightly, so we had to abandon them and turned to sandwiches. Though American food is not as delicately cooked as Chinese food, American food retains many nutrients just because of its rough preparation.

Most American students live off campus, some at home and others in rented apartments around the university. As university accommodation is very expensive, living off campus is a better choice as most of them support themselves by taking part-time jobs. All the students of the CSC-SUNY 150 Program lived on campus for convenience and safety. But we were also involved in some incidents, one of which was a fire alarm. The smoke of frying food in a shared kitchen triggered the fire alarm system, as a result all the students in the building had to evacuate the building in the sirens. Sometimes the fire drills would drive us out of the building whether it was noon, evening or midnight.

All the international students at the university are arranged with host families, and we were no exception. This is an activity organized by the international office for the international students to experience American culture and emerge in the American society. Every weekend, American host families would invite us to sightseeing, having dinners and visiting their families. Through all the activities, we experienced the authentic American life and gave the host families an opportunity to learn about the Chinese culture.

At Disneyland during winter break

The university also helped us in the application for a free commuter card for public transport, which entitled us to free ride on the public transport at Buffalo. So

we had the opportunity to visit many tourist destinations in this city, one of which is Niagara Falls between the USA and Canada. The weather was not so cold then and we boated into the fanciful and spectacular waterfall to feel its extreme grandeur and magic.

In addition, many students would take advantages of the vacations to go sightseeing and experience exotic features. In winter, some students went to Florida to enjoy the warm sunshine and beautiful beaches and had wonderful memories of the fireworks displayed in Disneyland; some went to Washington to pay respect to the American capital city, lingering in the museums around the Capitol Hill; some participated in Leadership Training Program and some even visited Canada to experience the busy and bustling life of another Northern American country. We have seen many unique American sceneries, experienced exotic cultures and customs, and broadened our vision.

Our Study

I still remember the first week when we came here and felt scared when we saw foreigners. I always felt out of place in a group of people with different colors. Above all, I could not understand the teachers in class, which gave me a lot of pressure. But later on, I adapted myself to this new life and could understand others and the teachers with only a few unknown words occasionally. With the nine months' study and experience, we felt obvious improvement in our listening comprehension and could even understand American films without subtitles. Zeng Xiutao, an English major from Southwest Jiaotong University who made a speech on behalf of the 150 students in the Consulate-General of the P. R. C. in New York, could speak standard American English now. One of the Buffalo State College teachers even joked that he should learn standard American pronunciation from this student.

Once the language barrier was overcome, we were very busy with our study. Every semester, we had to study for nearly the same number of credits, fewer than in China but we had to cope with frequent tests and exams in each subject. Everybody worked very hard to get an A. In spite of frequent tests, the difficult level was not very high, especially when we had a solid foundation for study. In the USA, we had no problem passing the exams, but it was no easy matter to get an A.

American students are very active in class, raising their hands to express opinions, and engaging in group discussions. The whole class is harmonious and lively and we learned a lot in such relaxing and delightful atmosphere.

We had to make appointments in advance with teachers due to their strong sense of time. Besides, in many offices such as university hospital and writing centers, one has to make appointments to get service. On the one hand, we feel that it is quite troublesome; on the other hand, we find it is more efficient to act according to rules.

On more than twenty campuses of SUNY, the students from Southwest Jiaotong University found themselves growing, experiencing and feeling the cultural differences. There are still many things waiting to be done. We'd like to extend our sincere thanks to the teachers, classmates and friends in the USA, who made us feel at home when we stayed in a foreign country; our thanks also go to the teachers and classmates at home whose care and concern accompanied us on the countless lonely nights and inspired us through the short and wonderful study period in the USA.

Xie Li, from Chongzhou City, Sichuan Province.

I study City Planning at Southwest Jiaotong University. In America, I studied at SUNY – Buffalo State College.

Those Memories Left Behind

By Zeng Xiutao
Southwest Jiaotong University

I have been back home for some days. During this time, without the habitual yelling and shouting of American students, the packing up before departure, and the reluctance in saying goodbye to my friends and teachers, after the fatigue from long-haul flight disappeared, I calmed down. Occasionally, I just sat there, recalling the trivial happenings when I was in the US—the curiosity when I just arrived there, feeling fresh, the simple pleasure I got when I was traveling, the slight sorrow when saying goodbye, the excitement when making speeches and the hearty laughter when teaching Chinese—All these have become beautiful memories, left behind in the USA, the other side of the Pacific Ocean.

I benefited a lot from the year in the US. Maybe some people say the greatest gain is the improvement in English, because the year has perfected my English, more idiomatic, more authentic, and more American. Indeed, my English has improved considerably, being able to communicate fluently with the Americans, and read the textbooks without consulting the dictionary. However, I don't think that is the greatest benefit; instead, it is the ability to practice introspect from the perspective of Western culture. Before going to the United States, I always felt that I had to be positive, forging ahead, without any pessimism. With this moral values, I gave myself a lot of pressure. In the United States, a strange environment to me, I found the American students very much enjoying their lives, most of whom would not strain themselves for any achievement. They are very practical: to buy a house with mortgage after graduation, or to be a primary school teacher, just simple ideals like this.

Later on, I began to ponder: in fact, I don't have to be somebody in the future; I only need to do something I like and enjoy myself. With the change of my ideas, I took a different attitude to my life. I used to feel nervous making public speeches, worried about making mistakes, now I still feel slightly nervous when making speeches, but not too much, and what is important is that I am not afraid of making mistakes, permitting myself to make occasional mistakes. This change of attitude has enabled me to perform better.

When we just arrived in the US, Peng Keyu, the Consul General in the Consulate-General of the P. R. C. in New York held a reception for us and I made a speech on behalf of all the students. Accordingly, I was made monitor when the seventeen of us arrived at Buffalo State College. It was the first time I was a monitor in the past

With the president of Buffalo State College

ten-odd years of study. So I was not very confident in this new role, dealing with matters in haste, fearing that I would not live up to the expectations of my classmates. Later on, I came to realize that there was no need to give myself so much pressure, and I became relaxed and slowed myself down, realizing that there should be stages and procedures in dealing with things and achieving goals step by step without worries or anxiety. It is very much like a long race; there is no need for us to dash to the finish line at high speed all the time, which may bring us a result to the contrary. Instead, we need to set a pace appropriate to our competence and fitness, and reach the finish line when we have picked up the speed and accumulated enough experience. With this awareness, I could manage to do things well with good rhythm such as the planning and organization of Mid-Autumn Festival dinner where we cooked some Sichuan food to thank the teachers for their care and concern for us, and the speeches I made at the farewell ceremony held by the President Howard of Buffalo State College and the board meeting...

Interviewing with Dr. Lee Ann Grace and Dr. Scott Johnson by Buffalo TV Station

On the night before we left New York, all the 150 university students spent an unforgettable night in the Consulate-General of the P. R. C. in New York with the teachers accompanying us to New York. Consul General Peng Keyu hosted a farewell party for us; presented at the meeting were all the 150 students and the teacher representatives from the twenty-two SUNY campuses. After the speeches and singing by Consul General Peng Keyu, Counselor Cen, and many other students, a sad feeling of having

Consul General Peng Keyu visiting Buffalo State College

to bid farewell diffused in the whole consulate, and many people could not help weeping. Cathy, my English teacher hugged me crying and saying that I am her Chinese son and I should go back to the US to visit her in the future and that she should have given me a key to her house as her house is my home. I promised her to go back to Buffalo to visit her and enjoy the black rice she is good at cooking...

I was deep in thought when the telephone rang and I was awoken to the reality in Chengdu. Looking at what I have written, I have to say that these beautiful memories have enriched my life, but I cannot take them away with me because they are left permanently on the land of the USA.

Holding love in our hearts, we are blessed to be given more.

Zeng Xiutao, from Pengzhou City, Sichuan Province.

I major in English at Southwest Jiaotong University. During my nine months in the US, I studied at SUNY − Buffalo State College.

My Life in an American University

By Chen Ling
Xihua University

May 12, 2008 has left a sad and tragic memory to all the Chinese. On this day, a massive earthquake which measured 8.0 on the Richter Scale killed thousands of people, and devastated beautiful cities and towns. Facing the disaster, we had to be strong. As a matter of fact, disasters make the nation strong and the country prosperous. All the Chinese united, and joined their efforts in disaster relief. In deep sorrow, we saw the courage and unity of the Chinese and the care and concern from peoples around the world. Many people made their donations and offered any possible help. We were unfortunate in being stricken by such a disaster and meanwhile we are fortunate in getting so much help. Just only month after the earthquake, the State University of New York invited 150 university students from the earthquake-hit area to study in SUNY for a year. With the help of government leaders and teachers, we arrived in New York on Aug. 15, a beautiful city I had been longing to see.

After a short stay in New York, I went with other sixteen students to SUNY – Buffalo State College. In Buffalo, you can find the sky very blue and feel the warm and very comforting breeze on your face. Upon our arrival at the dormitory, the staff of the international student accommodation prepared us the famous Buffalo chicken wings. I was amazed at this unexpected hospitality and found myself stammering when hearing their fluent and authentic English. After dragging my heavy luggage into my room, I lay on bed, no longer feeling any fatigue or discomfort.

On Aug. 25, the day on which the new semester officially began at

Buffalo State College, with slight nervousness, I walked into a strange classroom, met the American teacher and classmates. I felt frustrated in class with all the technical terms from the teacher. After class, I communicated with the teacher, who encouraged me to get involved in discussion and giving opinions. Gradually, I got familiar with my classmates, doing assignments and review together, and we became good friends. We also went to the library together to do reading or reviewing work. On many occasions when I came across a new word, they would stop to explain it to me. What impressed me most were the experimental classes in Chemistry course. My partner and I finished eleven experiments and we got very good grades in every experiment because of our harmonious cooperation and high efficiency. Apart from Chemistry, we seventeen Chinese students helped American students who were studying Chinese; consequently, Elisha became my good friend. We went together to shops and meals. As she liked Jay Chou's songs, I translated the words for her; I like American films, thus she took me to films in her car and she was my interpreter when I could not understand a certain word.

The class was lively, so was my life out of class. The college arranged a host family for each of us. A middle-aged couple Lynn and John entered my life. We went to dinner together, listened to music in church, went sightseeing in the city center. When they said that they were my American parents, I realized that I was homesick. With the rapid passage of time, Halloween came. We had a wonderful Halloween by

Fabulous Halloween

playing ghosts at home and giving out chocolates to children for Tricks or Treats. With Christmas approaching, Lynn and John prepared in advance some gifts for me, ready to give me a surprise on Christmas Eve. When I unpacked my gift, I found a metal snow flake with my name on it. John said it could remind me of Buffalo and their family after I went back to

China. Later Lynn gave me a delicate photo album, which recorded everything of our living together. It was time to say goodbye and I couldn't help crying. Lynn said that I was the best daughter in the world and I felt that she was the best American mother on earth. We did not want to

Happy smiles at Niagara Falls

part due to our close relationship; we know how to cherish because of pure friendship. I will always remember that departure is for meeting again.

We participated in a lot of extracurricular activities at the college, such as Asian Night, visits to the Niagara Falls, Washington and Toronto in Canada. All these made our lives interesting and rewarding.

At the end of the semester, at the home of the university president, the president presented us with certificates and souvenirs; we also became the Buffalo alumni of Grade 2009. With such high honors, we were

With the president of Buffalo State College and with certificates in our hands

very grateful to the governments of the two countries and to SUNY. Their joint efforts made possible our nine months' study in the US, thus the good memories. I felt happy with the care and concern of the teachers and we are fortunate to have met so many kind friends. All these will become my cherished memories and wealth.

Holding love in our hearts, we are blessed to be given more.

Chen Ling, from Pengzhou City, Sichuan Province.

I study in Chemistry Department, Xihua University. I studied at SUNY – Buffalo State College during my nine months in the US.

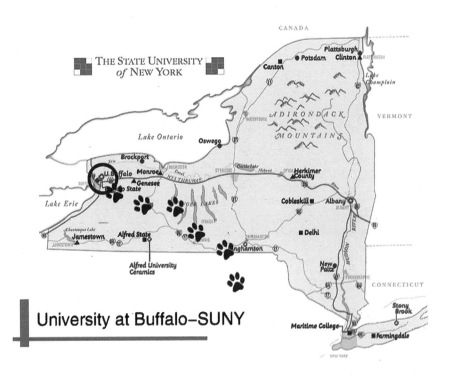

University at Buffalo–SUNY

My Footprints in the Past Year

By Ai Ling
Chengdu University of Technology

The year between 2008 and 2009 has flown away so fast. Time slipped but those happy and unforgettable memories remain.

During the year, so many people worked hard for us and sowed numerous seeds of altruistic love in us.

Also in the year, those seeds sprouted, sprang up, and opened their cheerful eyes, looking with curiosity at people and things around.

Last year, my friends and I arrived in the United States. For the first time in our life, we saw the baffling busy streets of New York City, the skyscrapers in Manhattan, and the characteristics of Chinese culture in China town. We were really impressed by the prosperity of US metropolises and the free and light atmosphere of American life.

August 16, 2008, in Manhattan

After two days' stay in New York, the 150 of us were placed on twenty-two of the SUNY sixty-four campuses. I was placed, together with Dai Ting (from Chengdu University of Technology), Ruan Tianyuan (from Sichuan University), and Yang Ran (from Southwest Jiaotong University), into the University at Buffalo – SUNY. On August

17, 2008, we flew from New York to Buffalo and began our year of overseas study in the United States.

Now talking about those days in the US, I would like to begin with my study. I majored in Chemical Engineering and had studied it in China for two years before I went to the US. Though I was not the best student, I could be more or less rated as one of full-growth students. Nevertheless, once at the University at Buffalo, the reputation I had built up as an excellent student fell down; for the course there was by no means a piece of cake as I had imagined. When I had overcome the language barrier and accustomed myself to the teaching modes, I came to realize that I had to work extremely hard and spend persistently twice as much time as my classmates on the course so as to catch up with them, or at least, not to lag too much behind them. Having had a bee in my bonnet for many a night, and having gone through the pressures and puzzles from study, I finally made great academic achievements. I was overjoyed with the rich fruits I had gained because I had tried, endeavored and strived. I felt no regret at my study over the past year.

Then, apart from my course, I managed to make my stay in the US as interesting and meaningful as possible. While experiencing American culture, I shared Chinese culture with my American teachers and friends. Such a cultural exchange promoted our mutual understanding of the other culture.

The first important festival I spent in the US was Thanksgiving Day. Invited by an American family, I joined them for the celebration that

November 26, 2008, Thanksgiving Day. From left to right: Lozana, me, her husband, their daughter and son.

day. I was cordially received. We sat around the dining table and listened quietly to the host's pious pray, hand in hand with our eyes gently closed. The whole house was filled with laughter that night; I saw sweet smiles on everybody's face. We had a joyful and unforgettable Thanksgiving Night together.

Later, I went to New Jersey and watched an NBA match—Rockets vs Nets. There were so many Chinese spectators because it seemed to be a match between Yao Ming and Yi Jianlian. The crowds were rather excited. In January, 2009, as a student of China 150, I participated in the Leadership Training Program held in Washington, D. C. During the six days, I took the opportunity to pay visits to some places of interest in Washington—such as the Capitol Hill, Kennedy Arts Center, and various museums and memorials. I learned a lot and widened my horizon a great deal.

March in Buffalo was still bitterly cold. Cold wind and heavy snow were everywhere. After two months, the much expected spring break had come at last. My friends and I would not waste the couple of days. We set forth for Los Angeles, California, to visit Disneyland and the Universal Studio there. After that, we headed for Las Vegas to be bewildered by the gambling city. Las Vegas is known in the world for three things—full of casinos, hockshops, and wedding chapels. The hotels there attract the world with their magnificent facades, exquisite interior decorations and layouts, which manifests the city's elegance, grace, luxury, etc. We ended up our journey by taking an intercity bus from Las Vegas to Arizona just to have a look at the Grand Canyon, one of the seven natural miracles on the globe. This journey was quite worth it. The Grand Canyon was so spectacular and lofty that we were knocked the breath of, daring not to move forward. I feared that was a painting whose coarse strokes might be revealed by a look at close distance. I feared that was a miracle which would vanish abruptly and completely. Moreover, I feared that was so much a hallucination of mine that any move might wake me up. All those were just my reverie. Such a canyon created by nature was a real thing; it stood there so grand, so imposing, and so towering....

May 15, 2009, farewell party

The short spring break was thus over. Now back at Buffalo, I had to resume my course. As the time for me to return to China was drawing near, I could not help feeling excited and sad. I was excited because I would soon be at my alma mater in my homeland and be reunited with my parents, my classmates, and my teachers. I was sad because I had come to love this beautiful and peaceful city. At Buffalo, so many people took good care of me, so many things touched me, and so much love from all around filled the year of my study at Buffalo with sweet memories. I would like to extend my thanks to all the members of Capen 411—the International Offices at the University at Buffalo. It was you who provided a new home for us who had been homeless after the big earthquake. You acted as our family members. I appreciate your listening patiently to our talks of hardships and happiness, your supervising our study like our parents, and your caring for our living at Buffalo. I will keep deep in mind your smiling faces, your affectionate hugs, your kind encouragements.

Finally, I would love to conclude that I obtained the knowledge of my specialty during the year in the United States. In the meanwhile, I had a deeper understanding of American culture and established close friendship with my American friends. However, the most important thing is that I have learned a saying—"Life is not only for us to learn but also for us to share and appreciate."

Life is not only for us to learn, but also for us to share and appreciate.

Ai Ling, from Dujiangyan City, Sichuan Province.

I study at Chengdu University of Technology. During my nine months in the US, I studied at University at Buffalo – SUNY.

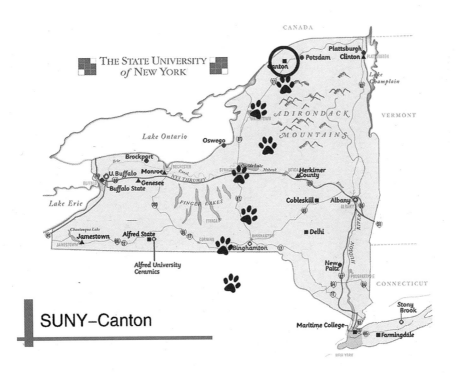

THE STATE UNIVERSITY
of NEW YORK

SUNY–Canton

Metamorphosis
—A Relation of My Nine-Month Study in the United States

By Zhang Guanghui
Southwest Jiaotong University

Time flew and the nine months has thus been over. I believe that many fellow students who joined in the CSC-SUNY 150 Program are likely to sigh with the same emotion. Comparing what I am now with what I was nine months ago, I have changed a lot. There are changes in me, great or small, perceptible or imperceptible. Whatever changes there may be, they are part of my growth. The recollections of this period in the United States are forever unforgettable because this experience has changed the course of my life inconspicuously.

I am not an ignorant freshman any more; but rather, I have become an elegant sophomore with a clear picture of my future. After the nine-month study in the USA, I have become fledged, vigorous and high-spirited.

I find I am much more confident now. I am proud not because I am a overseas returnee but because, having experienced so much, I have become sturdier and better acquainted with my own potential.

I find I have got a bit sentimental probably because I enjoyed so much care and love in the States. I am really thankful to all those who gave me care and love. I could not believe that a strong-minded man like me would burst into tears at the reception at the university Vice President's. Indeed, having gone through so many things, one could not but be moved when thinking back. The old Chinese saying goes: a man should never shed tears unless he is deeply moved.

I find I am mature now. My viewpoints are no longer naive, and my approaches to problems no longer simple. I have learned how to deal with

people and how to show love.

In short, I have really metamorphosed!

As a matter of fact, this program came to me quite unexpectedly. At that time, I thought it was too good an opportunity to lose. Then, I decided to try my best to win it.

It is often said that there are three types of people in the world. Type One are losers who are unprepared for any chance and regret bitterly when it is gone. Type Two are winners who can always seize any chance and succeed. Type Three are supermen who can create opportunities for themselves. I think I managed to be more than a winner this time. And I hope I can keep to be like this.

Thinking again and again about those nine months, I can see those happy moments moving in my mind like motion pictures.

From last July to the middle of last August, I was preparing for going abroad. I felt every day was passing so fast that I had to run after it. All of a sudden, I landed in the States as if I were having a dream. That was so quick and abrupt that I was at a loss from the very beginning. The problems it had caused me were by no means few. To start with, I had a problem with my English pronunciation, which I had neglected in my English learning in the previous years. In order to make my spoken English understood by others, I watched a lot of video programs and imitated the pronunciation. Before long, I was able to talk to natives with ease. Then, I began to yearn desperately for the tasty Sichuan food. I was served with western food day after day. At first, I found nothing wrong with it but I came to be tired of the small choice of tastes. Just a thought of the Sichuan style hotpot made me drool day and night. Things were not always so bad for we found a Chinese grocery store where we could buy some Chinese spices. We found it very interesting to cook for ourselves. Finally, I was hopelessly homesick. I called my mother every weekend to alleviate the agony arising from my nostalgia. However, over those phone calls, I learned more about my mother and appreciated more of her expectation of me. I swore not to let her down.

The teachers and staff at SUNY – Canton gave us many special treatments. We felt care and love everywhere. We are really grateful for what they have done for us. But for their care and love, we would not have enjoyed our stay in the States.

Pauline, the president's secretary who was in charge of the program at SUNY – Canton, was a kind "Mom." I still remember that, on leaving for China, all the six of us placed at Canton said to her, "We are your kids. We're going to see you again for sure." She treated us like her own kids. On the registration day, she

With Pauline at Grasse River

companied us all the way through our registration and took us to meals. That was of tremendous help to us who were totally strangers in the US.

She also organized birthday parties for all of us. To tell an interesting story, I had three birthday parties in the States during the nine months. The first one took place in our first week in the States. As the semester had not started yet, the teachers took us out for fun. After we had visited a number of places, we came to a restaurant called Friday for dinner. All the tables were occupied except a long one. I did not realize until later that it was reserved for birthday parties. The seat at the end was for the lucky guy whose birthday was to be celebrated. I did not know that; therefore, I took that seat. Just as I was busy eating the food I had ordered, a group of waiters and waitresses dressed in costumes burst at the table and placed a lovely small cake in front of me. In a moment, they started to sing sweet songs for birthday celebrations. I could not remember what they sang. The words they sang seemed that everybody was invited to celebrate the lucky guy's birthday. They sang so devotedly that some of the customers followed them. We could not help waving like conductors, and heard many people say, "Happy birthday!" In return, I kept saying thanks in English with a strong Chinese accent. Though it wasn't my birthday that day, I was still very excited for I was so lucky to have such an additional birthday.

That restaurant was very warm and considerate. When we were out, I asked my teachers why the restaurant did that for me. They told me it would had offered me the service no matter whether it was my birthday or not. That was its feature and tradition. This event shows that Americans are indeed clever business people.

Thanksgiving Day at Marela's

I had my second birthday celebration on October 9, 2008. Quite a number of the offices at Canton, including canteens and dormitories, kept the information of students' birthdays. It was not my birthday, either. My birthday is on October 9 according to Chinese lunar calendar; but, according to the solar calendar, it should be on November 22. However,

Celebrating birthday together with Zheng Miao

when I got to the canteen on the morning of October 9, the cashier greeted me with a big smile, "Happy birthday!" I was suddenly roused though I had been a little weary a moment before. I was rather happy and excited the whole day.

My third birthday party was given by my Mom Pauline. Zheng Miao, another participant of CSC-SUNY 150 Program, and I had our birthday parties at the same time because our birthdays were very close. Mom Pauline looked after us very well. Shortly after our arrival, she invited us to have grills at her home. She also took us to Chinese restaurants many a time. How lucky we were!

Another important "Mom" of ours was Marela, who was the director of International Programs at SUNY – Canton. Heading this program, she took care of us. We had a wonderful Thanksgiving Day at her home.

In the first semester, I also opted for some courses at St. Lawrence University, which they called "cross registration. " St. Lawrence University was a private university. It was so wonderful for me to attend classes simultaneously at two universities during my stay in the US. Thereby, I came to recognize the difference between private and state universities.

Private universities require more tuitions than state ones. Students at private universities can be classified into two groups: one group come from wealthy families; the other group are scholarship winners who used to be excellent high school teenagers.

Tutoring the kids of my host family to draw pictures during Christmas

SUNY – Canton is situated on the brim of a small town with Grasse River running by and thick woods surrounding it. Its campus was concealed by trees and plants, beautiful as a garden, with birds singing and flowers blossoming. Though smaller in size than my university (Southwest Jiaotong University) in China, SUNY – Canton accommodates more people. I guess there were a few thousands. There are many such small-size colleges in the States.

The first semester was just for us to adapt ourselves to the surroundings. However, even nine months was far from enough. Despite of that, we began to enjoy American life after the first semester. We had no more trouble talking with people, and had acquired more knowledge of American culture, geography, economy, politics, and so on.

What was important was the winter break after the first semester. I spent it at my host family. This is a typical American family—a two-story house, a couple, a number of children, and a relationship full of love and affection among the family members. It was Christmas when I got to the family. The whole house had been nicely decorated. They treated me with great hospitality stemmed from the bottom of their hearts. This is a harmonious family and its members love each other. I was so envious of this family that I wanted to set up a similar one for myself in the future.

I found a part-time job in a restaurant in the second semester. The job taught me the hardships of working and how to make money. Nevertheless, each time I got my paycheck, I was very happy. I had learned the importance of earning one's own bread with one's own hands.

We established a Chinese club last semester, and in the first week of this semester we organized a Spring Festival party in its name. Together, we went shopping, prepared food, decorated the hall, and rehearsed our performances. We were spreading Chinese culture, serving as cultural ambassadors.

Now I am back in my motherland, China. There are still many people in need of help and a lot of work to be done. Now that I am back, it's high time I gave and returned.

The only limitation to your success is your imagination.

Zhang Guanghui, from Mianyang City, Sichuan Province.

I study Civil Engineering at Southwest Jiaotong University. During my nine months in the US, I studied at SUNY – Canton.

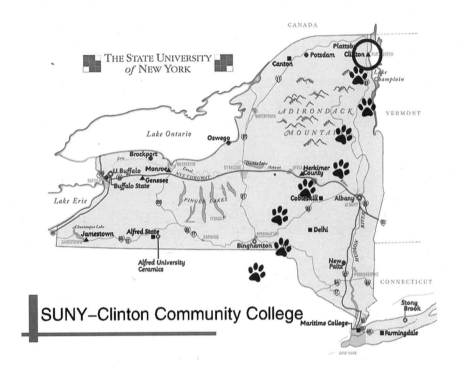

THE STATE UNIVERSITY
of NEW YORK

CANADA

Plattsb
Potsdam Clinton ▲ PLATTSBURGH
Canton   Lake
                                    Champlain

                    VERMONT

ADIRONDACK
Lake Ontario   WATERTOWN
Oswego   MOUNTAI

Brockport   Eric
U.Buffalo Monroe   SYRACUSE   Oneida Lake
Genesee   NYS THRUWAY   UTICA Herkimer
Buffalo State   County
Lake Erie   Cobleskill   Albany
                                              ALBANY
          FINGER LAKES
Chautauqua Lake   ITHACA
Jamestown Alfred State   Delhi
                    CORNING
                    BINGHAMTON
         Alfred University   Binghamton
         Ceramics   New
                                       Paltz
                                              POUGHKEEPSIE
                                                    CONNECTICUT

SUNY–Clinton Community College   Stony
                                                  Brook

                    Maritime College
                                    Farmingdale
                        NEW YORK

The Clips of My Visit to the United States

By Qiang Tao
University of Electronic Science and Technology of China

Summer

I arrived in New York in August, 2008. It was a golden season with golden maple leaves everywhere...

Everything in New York City appeared fancy to us who had just come to this land. After a short stay in NY, we were dispatched separately to various campuses of SUNY. On our way, we were curious about everything we saw and full of expectations like newly born babies. To our surprise, we were received with kindness and warmth given by our American friends. The first thing we did after our arrival was to join our American teachers in a BBQ. Although my favorite chilli wasn't available at the American-style BBQ, I was very happy to be with the affable teachers and staff members for the first meeting, and enjoyed the sweet American BBQ sauce. While we were having our BBQ, two deer came out of the woods nearby, playing leisurely and cheerfully. The teacher sitting by me told me that they were wild deer coming to say hello to us. Our first night at SUNY − Clinton Community College passed with BBQ, wild deer, and hospitable American teachers. It was a lovely mid-summer night—fresh, novel, and exciting, making me look forward to my upcoming campus life there.

Fall

As maple leaves were getting redder and redder, late fall could be more and more strongly felt in New York. The curiosity was being replaced by the tension from study.

Thirty years ago, many Chinese went abroad to study what they were unable to learn at their homeland, whereas it is now more probable that we go abroad to experience different teaching modes. Here at SUNY, the design and contents of its courses were more or less the same as those at my university at home, but what were different were the teaching modes.

In the classes at my university in China, teachers lectured on the platforms while the students generally listened silently in their seats. On the contrary, the classes in the US were filled with light-heartedness and briskness. Moreover, there were more interactions between teachers and students. At first, I was by no means used to the American classes: the professors were frequently interrupted by the students who raised their hands to put forward their points of view, to ask questions, and even to disagree with the professors. However, the professors were always happy to answer the students' questions. (Professors in the US love those students who love asking questions for they believe quiet students do not have much potential.) Very often a class turned out to be an exchange of ideas between professors and their students. At the beginning, I was afraid of asking questions in classes because I had not done that for years. And I was also afraid I might ask very silly questions. Nonetheless, in classes as such, nobody would think your questions were meaningless; on the contrary, it was a fundamental learning attitude to ask questions zealously. The effects of such classes became better because students would be more attentive in free and active classes. I changed gradually in the course of my study at SUNY and became active in asking questions and joining in discussions in classes. And I found I had gained a lot in the mean time. Fall should be a season of rich fruits.

Winter

New York in winter was covered with snow all over. The bitter cold made it difficult for me to adapt myself to the uncomfortable climate, but coming along with the coldness was my first break in the US. I had expected it for a long time because there were so many places I had expected to visit in NY. Given a drive by a kind American teacher, my classmates and I went to New York City. "Read hundreds of volumes of books; Travel thousands of miles of roads" (a Chinese proverb which encourages learning). There are things you cannot learn from books. You had to learn them through your own experiences. We marveled at so many things in New York: the United Nation's headquarters, the Metropolitan Museum of Art, Wall Street, Central Park, etc.

Those dazzling things amazed us so much that we realized that the world was indeed very enormous—so enormous a stage that we could perform a great deal on it. We should not have looked down upon ourselves; but rather, we were always far stronger than we had ever imagined us to be. If we looked farther and higher, all the difficulties that had seemed insurmountable would become much smaller. The New York in cold winter was still attractive and brilliant.

Spring

New York's early spring was characterized by wild cold winds. However, with the help of my American teachers, I got my first job in my life—a student assistant of International Office, SUNY – Clinton Community College. It was a nice job and the payment was very good (10 dollars an hour). This job sounded fussy but was in effect simple. I learned from my job more about American youths, viz. their independence. I was particularly impressed with their independence. Most American college boys and girls have their own jobs. They get independent at early ages of their parents' financial supports. Except for

We stayed in our president's home for Thanksgiving Day; this is the picture with the president and his wife.

their tuition fees, they are usually able to support themselves, and many of them keep several jobs at the same time. Compared with them, I had had very little true social experience. Nevertheless, I had started in the US to seek for more. At the end of spring in New York, I got my first pay. With 300 dollars in hand, I felt very great.

From the spring through the winter, each of the four seasons in New York was excellent and substantial, never devoid of smiles. When the next summer was approaching, it was time for us to say goodbye to the four seasons that had just passed. With full backpacks, home we went.

Reading hundreds of volumes of books;
Travelling thousands of miles of roads.

Qiang Tao, from Mianzhu City, Sichuan Province.

I study Software Engineering at University of Electronic Science and Technology of China. During my nine months in the US, I studied at SUNY − Clinton Community College in the first semester in America, then I transferred to Stony Brook University in the second semester, majoring in Computer Science.

In Praise of Love

By Li Junchen

Southwestern University of Finance and Economics

As one of the China 150, I was lucky to come to SUNY − Clinton Community College.

The days at Clinton Community College were happy and eventful: the joyful barbecue party by the lake, the bravery in battling with ice and snow in the mountains in winter, the great care the teachers gave to us in class, the cooperation in fulfilling our assignments, the learning of making American food at friends' homes, the agitation in arguing about political

With Ashley and Adam after watching a hockey game in Plattsburgh State

issues, the help and privities in physical education classes, the excitement at ceremonies, the experience of Western culture.... All those sweet memories are printed in my mind for the rest of my life.

However, it was the teachers that touched me most. I was often touched to tears by their considerateness and love. Their love was so unselfish, so straightforward, so natural, and so genuine. It was the kind of love I had never witnessed and I myself had not yet possessed, but now it has become part of my life.

Diane, our English teacher, lectured on American culture to us in the first semester. She was always smiling and answering our questions patiently. When I had a sore shoulder out of an old injury, she gave up her leisure hours and took me to the hospital for a check. Later, she spent a lot of time helping me with the bills. When I did not have enough money for my tour, she lent it to me. When I asked if she wanted an IOU, she looked at me like a mother and said, "No, Charles. I trust you." At that moment, my heart quivered with emotion because I had never come across such kindness and trust. Diane also offered to take us to

Diane and her husband put on their Chinese costumes for us at the farewell barbecue.

Boston and Quebec for fun. Later she told me that, when she was a student at Austria, her teacher had often taken her and his other students out for journey. According to her, her Austrian teacher loved his students very much and took the opportunity of travelling to teach them the meaning of travel. He had also taught them how to enjoy travel at the lowest cost and how to discover the beauty of the world by means of travel. Now that Diane was a teacher herself, she was determined to pass this instruction and love onto her students. We benefited a great deal from her encouragement and love which accompanied us all the way through our journeys. She told us the history of Vermont. She often reminded us to put on our hats in the rain. We were scampering about on the ferry like kids, but she watched us with smiles like an amiable mother. I wondered if the sides of the Charles River could have been so beautiful without her company! If I could be a teacher myself some day, I would do as Diane did—love my students and teach them to be honest, friendly, kind and happy. I would take them out for outings, for journeys, and for admiring the charm of nature and human wisdom.

There were so many teachers and students on the campus. No matter whether they knew each other or not, they always greeted and smiled at each other. Moreover, before I asked for help, I was always asked, "Can I help me?" Though I spent five months of ice and snow in Plattsburgh, I felt warm, peaceful and pleased all the time. I appreciated the people here. I learned a lot—honesty, friendliness, and earnestness, all of which will benefit me for the rest of my life.

We came in fall in August, and we are leaving in early summer in May. We will bring with us the love and care our American friends gave us. Back in our homeland, we will be volunteers and enable the children in the areas hit by the big earthquake to live a happier life. We will help with the reconstruction with all our might. We will learn more earnestly and reconstruct our lovable motherland because we now are able to offer love.

I will remember the year we were cultivated by our American friends. Their efforts will be passed on and widely spread.

I always remember my happy life in Clinton. People here have given me a lot. Thank you! I will spread the love to more people in China, and in the world.

Li Junchen, from Jiangyou City, Sichuan Province.

I study Financial Statistics at Southwestern University of Finance and Economics. In America, I went to SUNY – Clinton Community College. I love maths, science, history, and sports.

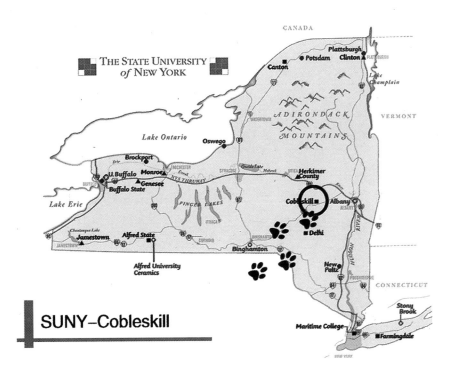

THE STATE UNIVERSITY
of NEW YORK

CANADA

Plattsburgh
Potsdam   Clinton
Canton

Lake
Champlain

ADIRONDACK

VERMONT

MOUNTAINS

Lake Ontario   Oswego

Brockport

ROCHESTER
U.Buffalo   Monroe   SYRACUSE   Oneida Lake   Mohawk   UTICA   Herkimer
NYS THRUWAY   County
Genesee
Buffalo State

Lake Erie   FINGER LAKES   Cobleskill   Albany

ITHACA   ALBANY

Chautauqua Lake   Alfred State   CORNING   Delhi   HUDSON RIVER
Jamestown
JAMESTOWN   Binghamton   BINGHAMTON

Alfred University
Ceramics

New
Paltz
CONNECTICUT

Stony
Brook

SUNY–Cobleskill

Maritime College   Farmingdale

NEW YORK

A Year Saturated with Love
—A Personal Account of My Nine-Month Study in the US

By Chen Linglong
Sichuan University

Arrival

Having flown for fourteen hours, we—the second group of China 150 young adults from the earthquake-hit area of Sichuan—landed at last in the United States of America. It was around 10 p. m. when we arrived at the John F. Kennedy International Airport. After claiming our baggage, we set off for SUNY – Maritime College by bus. In the depth of night, the shades of night were a bit cold and lights were scattered in distance. As the bus was running on the highway with green trees on both sides whizzing by, I suddenly felt as if I were still riding on our university bus in Chengdu.

We must be close to our destination now because we could see houses after houses on either side of the road. There were yards in front of and behind those houses, on the tops of which the Stars and Stripes were tilted. Cars were parked near the front doors. That was my first impression of the United States.

Though we reached the campus at midnight, the college had prepared dinner for us. With a knife, a fork, and a plate in hand, I realized again I was on a foreign land. There was no chilli, no rice; but salads and bread instead.

In the next days we did a number of things. First of all, we ate at Golden Bridge Restaurant where we enjoyed delicious food and were warmly greeted by people from my homeland. Thereby, we felt less

lonely in a foreign country. Then, we went to Battery Park where the deep blue sea and the skyscrapers made us feel differently. Finally, we paid a visit to Consulate-General of the People's Republic of China in New York. There was no need to mention its grandeur and stateliness. We met the teachers from the SUNY colleges in a hall, which was decorated in Chinese style with its floor covered with a heavy floral carpet. We 150 young adults were about to start with our different experiences—what was there awaiting us? We were looking forward to it curiously.

Then we got on the college buses separately and waved farewell to the center of New York. On the journey to our college, we were impressed by the green fields and elated by the beauty of nature. SUNY − Cobleskill was set in a small town called Cobleskill. In what was known as upstate New York lay undulant small hills, on which stood tall conifers. Beautiful horses, cute sheep and small houses were dotted all over the hills. This scene upset our imagination of New York. Perhaps to many Chinese, New York must be related with skyscrapers, big busy streets, and crowds of people. Many Chinese often mix up New York City with New York State. However, the eastern part of New York State is totally different. People here lead a peaceful rural life and enjoy the beautiful scenes of nature.

Sitting alone in my dorm, I found it very quiet all around. I began to guess what my roommate would look like, and how we could get along with each other. I grew excited about that. Back in China, when I was applying to join in this program, I just wanted to have a try. Now I was right here on the land many Chinese desire to set foot on.

Some Anecdotes

Our program officer at SUNY − Cobleskill was an old urbane man called Jonathan who was about sixty years old. We called him "Grandpa" respectfully.

We met him for the first time at Consulate-General of the P. R. C. in New York when he went there with the president to pick us up. He was very tall with a silvery whisker. He looked a bit serious and never smiled like others when speaking. My first impression of him was that he was not amiable. I had not seen his first smile until he called my name and handed my room key over to me on the Cobleskill Campus.

At Jonathan's house before leaving for home

Jonathan took care of us and always made perfect arrangements for details we had failed to think of. I can still remember that he always sat in a chair in front of our dormitory, a cup of coffee in hand, waiting for us. He accompanied us through our registration, our option for classes, and our purchase of books; and gave us instructions whenever necessary. He ate with us, bought us boots and heavy clothes when winter was coming, and encouraged us to go to the Mid-Autumn Festival party when we were invited by the local Chinese Association in Albany. He even made plans for our tour to Florida....

One day, one of us told him that we would give him a nickname. He asked curiously what it was. Then my classmate asked him to allow us to call him "Grandpa" and explained its meaning in Chinese to him. Thus we got closer and friendlier with him. Each time we went out, Grandpa Jonathan would call the roll for there were eighteen of us. At another

My Halloween making-up

outgoing shortly before we were to return to China, he called the roll again. He said, "I'll call the roll till I see all of you off for China. " He called the roll again a month before we left for China. We all started to count down but Grandpa Jonathan told us that he had started to count down on the 139th day after our arrival. We calculated with our fingers—he had started to count down on January 1, 2009. We all became silent at that moment....

Day after day, with the help and care of all the people around, we constantly grew up and learned a lot not only from books. We concentrated so long on our study that we neglected many things. For example, we forgot to communicate with our families and friends. Yet over here in Cobleskill, our hearts would be warmed with the short greetings from the people we knew.

We worked on our courses with the diligence and surefootedness we had brought with us from China. Nevertheless, apart from our courses, there was a lot for us to learn and experience.

To study a course is not only to acquire knowledge but to grow up as well. I can never forget the module named Wetland Appraisal & Assessment. It took me much trouble to be admitted to module. It could never be done without the help of my tutor. The code of this module started with the figure 3, which represented a junior one. In principle, we were advised not to opt for junior courses for fear that we might have language barriers.

In the first few sessions, Professor Losito spoke so fast that I could hardly catch up with him. However, I stayed with him because I believed that only by this could I make great progress.

Florida trip during winter break

This module called for lab assignments. Each time we had to go to wetland like mires and swamps to do the lab work. That reminded me of the Red Army's going over wetland more than half a century ago. I could understand the hardships they had gone through. Stepping in mires, I was once stuck in the mud and had to be pulled out by my classmates. Each time I was back in our dorm, I had to scrub my shoes because they were filled with muck. Those assignments were never suspended by winds and rains. It would be rather embarrassing for me to hold an umbrella in the rain because none of my classmates did that. It would be troublesome, too. How I admired my classmates who were quick and efficient in action, not caring about being dirty and tired!

Working on this module, I also felt my teacher's tender care. Once in mountains and forests, he was apt to introduce to us a lot of things beyond our course such as things about salamanders and turkeys. He wanted us to learn more. (Our module was chiefly of botany.) It was via this module that I dared to put a lizard on my palm or let a snake wind around my arm for the first time in my life. When the days were getting colder, the teacher would always tell us to put on more clothes and boots to prevent cold water. English was no longer a barrier for me because the teacher had thought out the solution before I could. He advised me to look for some translation machine in the library.

A variety of activities in those nine months broadened my horizon. These include Leadership Training Program, meeting the First Lady of New York State, the various events organized by the International

Students' Club such as international foods contest, the Russian movie festival, visits to movie houses, the trip to Boston, etc.

Then something interesting happened in last autumn break. I came to know Americans' view of history. Compared with China which has a history of a few thousand years, the United States is indeed a young nation. Americans usually seemed energetic and outgoing to me, not like us Chinese who tended to be more self-controlled. Hence, I wondered what a viewpoint the American nation had of history. At this time of the season, the Chinese nation was celebrating its national day; whereas we did not feel that right here in the United States. An American friend of mine invited us to visit her; so I went to her family with some humble gifts. She has a big family, and I could feel a deep love between the family members. Her cousins were all gifted: some were great singers and others good pianists. An embroidered piece caught my eyes. It was a work of her grandfather's mother. The words on it read:

Dear house
You are really very small
Just big enough
To hold the love

Those yellowish old photos and finely-made spoons—The spoons were left to Grandpa Dave by his mother, and hung on the wall as decorations—veraciously suggested to me the American cultural basis and their attitude toward history.

Conclusion

I encountered many first things in my life during the days in the US: my first stay on a foreign land, my first view of sea, my first drift on a river, my first ride on the subway train, my first lizard's catching, my first being stuck in mud, my first poem recitation on the stage, my first visit to NBA match, my first wearing scarf in April, my first hitchhiking, etc.

This experience in the US enabled me not only to learn from books and improve my English but also to learn how to value and love others in return.

This nearly one year was filled with love. The 150 kids of us were embraced and watered by love. We are all ambitious now and hope to give other people as much of our help as we possibly can, to love others in return, and to spread love far and wide—for great love knows no boundary.

Chen Linglong, from Wenchuan County, Aba Tibetan and Qiang Autonomous Prefecture.

I enrolled in Sichuan University in 2006, studying Environmental Science in Architecture and Environmental Department. I got the chance to study at SUNY – Cobleskill on August 15, 2008.

My American Teacher Mark

By Li Jin
Sichuan Agricultural University

It was my happiest year: I did not have to worry about my living; and worry concealed itself like a bird in winter and raised its timid head only occasionally.

Now the "United States" on the other side of the globe is rather a land I always care about than a spatial concept in my mind. The stories about those people and those things are by all means endless. However, I would like to tell you about one of the many adorable people—my teacher, Mark.

Fishing by electro fishing boat

My major was Fishery and Aquaculture which deals mainly with fish diseases and fish drugs. I majored in the same in the United States. Very few college girls would choose this major. Each time I told people about my major, they would stare at me with their eyes wide open and say "cool." However, a college girl as I was, I was not at all treated differently. Even my teacher Mark treated me like male students. So far I wonder if you have formed the following picture of my teacher in your mind: an old man in his sixties, a pair of glasses on his austere face, a pair of piercing eyes that will cripple your youth's pride. Nevertheless, that was not Mark.

Mark was actually very young, aged thirty-six and childless. He himself often behaved like a kid. Whenever I asked him questions, he always tilted his head to one side, pouting and gazing at me rakishly. He would not answer me till I stammered out my questions. In class, he would turn suddenly and stylishly around, and use the red light to point at the keynotes he had written on the whiteboard. Sometimes, he sat on a desk while speaking, supporting himself on both hands on the desk, both of his feet hanging and swaying like pendulums. When we were doing lab, he was the head of the fishing group and was more excited than his students at the fish floating on the water stunned by electricity. The tranquility of the lake was immediately broken by his shouting. He was blaming, urging and telling us where there were fish afloat. He was flourishing on the boat. Could anyone not be stirred up by his enthusiasm and take no action? Our boat was always loaded with laughter and holler.

However, Mark's considerateness was not overshadowed by his big boy's candor. Each of us was required to make a presentation at the end of the semester. The presentation was to be held at noon. Mark prepared a large pan of delicious food for us all by himself for fear that we might miss our lunch. Beside the pan, loaves of bread, butter, and potato chips were

neatly arranged. I knew Americans did not like chilli but he deliberately brought some along. I knew it was especially prepared for me though he did not say it. He was such a sprightly and lovable teacher that his lectures were conceivably vivid and interesting.

After two semesters, I

Scenery on the way to the lab

had appreciated many splendid views of the American countryside by taking advantage of the short trips for my lab.

Much of the work for my major was done off campus. Mark lectured very little. After he had given very brief instructions, we took our tools and rushed in our car to lakes, rivers, or streams. On those trips, we saw beautiful villages, vast prairies, and hills covered with refreshing green. Roads meandered in woods. Here and there a steep slope sprang up in front of our car as if we were bumping along a roller coaster. When we reached open stretches, we saw railed ranches. Herds of cattle were grazing, lying on the ground, or standing casually. I always leaned against the car window, looking out silently. I could not quite catch people's talks because of my poor English; so I turned to my eyes and my heart for the understanding of the world. In contrast to my reticence, my classmates held jolly talks in the car. Those seated in front of me would have heated arguments with Mark over certain issues; and those behind me would sit close, chatting about recent happenings. In this narrow enclosure everybody removed the distance between each other and opened his or her heart, friendly greetings vibrating the air. Unlike in a large classroom, this closeness led each of us to get to know the people around. After several such trips, we all became bosom friends.

This picture was taken when we did ice fishing survey on Otsego Lake; people in the picture were my classmates.

Yet the lab work itself was not so easy. Even in cold winter, our trips were never stopped by wind and snow. We often had to put our hands into freezing cold water in rivers to gather some invertebrates which were buried in mud or sand. In case we wetted our sleeves out of carelessness, we would shiver with cold when we got out of the rivers. Each lab session usually lasted for four hours. If we slept late sometimes, we would not have time for breakfast; therefore, we would go hungry the whole morning. In early spring, when snow still lay a few feet thick, we had to do some ice fishing survey. The bitterly cold wind cut our ungloved hands like a sharp knife. In addition, though sometimes hungry, we had to walk around for one or two hours, asking people questions. When the survey was over, we had normally been so starved as if our heads were haunted by numerous humming flies. There were still tents scattered over the snow-covered ground. It seemed that those people who were keen on ice fishing did not care about strong winds and heavy snows. Even if they caught nothing that day, they still appeared self-content. That was the most primitive psychology of hunting—putting themselves into the arms of mother nature without impatience and complaint. Once close to mother, everyone would be at ease. Later on, I came to understand the reason why Mark had never asked how I felt: since you love fish and nature, you have to embrace earth and coldness and accept the strong fishy smell.

My heart captured the friendliness my ears and eyes failed to. Mark would praise me for any small achievement in class. He was the kind of teacher who would not offer you a hand immediately when you were struggling but who would smile at you when you had groped through darkness. Yet you were aware that he was just there with you but he never intervened more than necessary. He only wanted you to learn how to stand on your own feet.

As for the boys in my class, they always seemed careless. I thought they were stone-hearted like that for good. However, shortly before I returned to China, Mark requested me to make a presentation on Sichuan and China. It took me three whole weeks to prepare for the presentation. In my last class, I successfully presented the resplendent Chinese culture and language to my American classmates. When I glimpsed over the classroom, I caught sight of two familiar faces. They had attended the same lectures in the previous semester with me. To my surprise, they came to my presentation. And after my presentation, they gave me two exquisite photo frames which recorded the days we spent together. They told me the frames were presents for me to take back to China. I smiled heartily to them because the frames were the most precious things I got in those nine months.

Days go on and on. Now the sun shines at me and them in turn. I would like to ask the sun to extend my sincere blessing to those lovable people in Cobleskill when it turns to their side. May my blessing be melted into the sunshine that it will always shine onto them!

The whole world's darkness can not crush out the light of a little candle; light ourselves and others with love.

Li Jin, from Deyang City, Sichuan Province.

I study Fishery and Aquaculture at Sichuan Agricultural University. In America, I studied at SUNY – Cobleskill. One of the sentences by Benjamin Franklin strikes me: Honesty and diligence should be your friends forever. My ultimate goal is to make the countryside better and improve farmers' living standard and self-cultivation.

Sichuan, We're Coming Back

By Yuan Yuan
Southwest Jiaotong University

My baggage had been packed up. While the others were still busy choosing what to be packed and what to be left behind, I was sitting in the empty bedroom, staring at nowhere. As a child from the earthquake-stricken area of Sichuan Province, in the past nine months, I had experienced much and got a lot from the fertile land of the United States. And now, I was about to come back to Sichuan, my hometown that experienced so heavy a blow but still remained strong. Full of exhilaration, I started to pack my belongings one week earlier, unwilling to leave the United States, though. I opened the packed baggage, taking things out and putting them in again and again. I hoped to bring back all that I had gained from the States, but had to throw away lots of them. Saying goodbye is something sorrowful.

With eighteen students and thirty-six suitcases on it, the bus began to move slowly. Inside the bus, someone could not help weeping, and then another one burst into tears. At this, my eyes became wet, but I tried my best to restrain my tears; though I, like the others, was so reluctant to leave this beautiful land, Cobleskill. It is so beautiful! The tree leaves are as green as what we saw the moment we arrived. I tried my utmost to keep in my memory every scenic spot and every part of the place! Life is short! Is it possible for me, in my lifetime, to come back to meet again all those who have loved and cared for us?

While the bus was moving on, I said goodbye to every familiar building that came into view.

Porter Hall—our dormitory. Every morning when we woke up, I

would lie in bed, appreciating the picturesque scenery outside the window while pondering quietly. In my view was a colorful mountain, which would become white with the advent of winter. Whenever I was lonely or nostalgic, I would look out, and the big mountain would make me feel great and tolerant, thus forgetting all my loneliness. In the small irregular bedroom of the dorm, I used to sit up late until the early morning, studying, video-chatting with my family, practicing calligraphy with my friends or playing cards with my foreign friends. My dormitory is my haven, small but cozy, filled with love.

Champlin Hall—our canteen. I have been to quite a few campuses of the State University of New York. I feel proud to tell other classmates of mine on other campuses that the food on the Cobleskill Campus is the most delicious! The cooks in the International Bar of the campus prepared rice specifically for us Chinese students. When we just arrived, lettuce salad and the like did not cater to our taste, so it was wonderful to eat a bowl of rice with soy sauce which is typically used in Chinese cooking. Afterwards, the considerate cooks always prepared international food for international students every week, and therefore I had an opportunity to taste different types of food from many countries. In Champlin Hall, I had an affectionate "mother," a middle-aged woman. I called her Mom because she regarded me as her daughter, a daughter whose smile was what she liked best. Every morning, I would eat egg dishes cooked by her. She frequently brought me Chinese dishes and gave me a lot of American souvenirs. When I felt ill, she would buy me electuary or syrup of Traditional Chinese Medicine. I have never been to her home; however, I know she does not lead a rich life, she is a happy, affectionate and broad-minded woman. I am a lucky girl to have met her, and I would like to extend my sincere gratitude and give my best blessings to her.

Knapp Hall—I have the most beloved "Grandfather" here. When we just arrived at Cobleskill, the elderly man taking care of us held a meeting and asked us to make any possible demand when it occurred. The kind-hearted Grandpa just did not want us to feel self-abased, telling us that we may have whatever American students have. Deeply touched, we began to address him "Grandpa." Since then, Grandpa had meals with us, and took care of our study and living, etc. Grandpa would be ready to help the eighteen Chinese students when any need should arise. He always felt proud, telling others that the Cobleskill Campus, though quite small, accommodated the second largest number of students from the CSC-SUNY 150 Program. Actually, none of us eighteen Chinese students had ever thought that we could establish such profound friendship with this American Grandpa. After we came back to China, Grandpa was the one we would miss most!

The Gym—Isn't there anything special about it since every campus has one? Yes, there is. A lot of recollections! Every weekend we would play badminton, volleyball or basketball there. I had been a person having no taste for athletics at all; however, I could be seen right in the gym every weekend evening. My playmates would just play with me, without caring whether I played well or not. Every time I had a very good time, playing until my gym suit was all wet. The gym is a symbol of our solidarity, recording happiness of us eighteen students on the Cobleskill Campus. In October of 2008, when we just arrived at Cobleskill, we had a calligraphy contest with the Japanese students. It was said that the Japanese students accounted for the biggest percentage of the overseas students before we arrived. Every time they had a calligraphy performance, Americans would very much appreciate it. Some Japanese even claimed that calligraphy was a treasure of Japanese culture. We showed the American students our calligraphic capability, proving that the art actually belongs to the Chinese culture.

The Warner Hall—I learned every subject of mine in this very teaching building. Different professors of the ten subjects taught us in a totally different way from the Chinese one, and we gained a lot from their teaching. At the very beginning of the semester, every week there must be quite a few exams, so I studied at high pressure as if I had come back to my senior high school life. By and by I became accustomed to the learning method and even began to love it. At the end of the semester I got straight A for all the subjects!

Now the bus was driving out of the school. Goodbye, Cobleskill! The students on the bus all burst into tears, words failing to express our unwillingness to leave. I asked myself, "Has my dream in the United States come to an end?" At the moment, more scenes came to my memories.

At Thanksgiving, three classmates of mine and I went to Boston. To save money, we planned to spend the first night on the bus. But due to the schedule change of the buses on the holidays and failure to book a room beforehand, we got to Boston earlier than we had planned and spent the night on the street. It was an unforgettable and sleepless night: we wondered about to three stations, and were even followed by people with evil intentions. It was my first self-planned travel! Although it was not well-planned, I learned a lot from it.

On Christmas Eve, we went to New Jersey to see an NBA game, which many people were eager to watch, because Yao Ming from Houston Rockets would play against another Chinese player, Yi Jianlian, from New Jersey Nets. Then I stayed in New York for one week, appreciating this world-famous metropolitan city: Central Park, Times Square, Broadway, the Wall Street, the Fifth Avenue, etc. The bigger the city is, the smaller I feel I am in this world!

In January, Grandpa took us eighteen children to travel around Florida. We had a barbeque party at the beach, played beach volleyball, rode a yacht, went to the Disneyland, and traveled around Florida. It was the first time for us eighteen students from the Sichuan Basin to see a sea! We felt very excited, jumping and running about. Meanwhile, I felt I became much more broad-minded!

In April, my classmates and I went to travel for the second time. We travelled from Philadelphia to Baltimore, then to Washington, New Jersey and finally to New York City. With much travel experience, our travel this time was very smooth. We were in time to see the Easter Day Parade held in New York City.

Afterwards, Liu Yandong, the State Councilor, led a group to see us from our motherland. We eighteen students, out of the 150 children from the Sichuan earthquake-stricken area, read out for them a poem entitled "We Have a Strong Motherland." The performers and the audience alike were moved to tears. The earthquake could take away our family members or relatives, but our power and spirit would remain!

In May, we 150 students from the earthquake-stricken area were about to leave the United States for Sichuan, and would use what we had learned from America to serve our motherland. We have no doubt about ourselves, because we, after a year's overseas study, are more mature both physically and psychologically. We will not feel hesitant because we have more confidence in ourselves. There is every reason for us to believe the world and everybody beside us. We will shed tears not because we feel sad but because we are happy. Sichuan, China, we're coming back!

Treat life with your heart. Learn to appreciate. Learn to love!

Yuan Yuan, from Chongzhou City, Sichuan Province.

I study Accounting at Southwest Jiaotong University. During my nine months in the US, I studied at SUNY - Cobleskill.

117

Gratitude and Responsibility

By Tang Ji
Southwestern University of Finance and Economics

Facing the computer screen, I began to write about my experience in the United States. My thoughts went back to the moment when the airplane landed at the Kennedy Airport in New York on August 15, 2008. Lots of things happened in the hundreds of days and nights during my stay in the United States. Though lacking linguistic talent of expressing my gratitude in my heart, I would like to tell the folks in my hometown that we were all very well and that we were trying our best to study hard and learn something.

During the year, what I learned here is gratitude. Now I was about to leave this land, but I was really reluctant to say goodbye to my American friends. We eighteen Chinese students studied at SUNY – Cobleskill. The college of the State University of New York (SUNY) is situated in a small town near Albany, the capital city of New York State. The teachers here treated us as their own children, helping us with our study, and taking us out

With Grandpa and Grandma at Cobleskill. They treat us as their family members.

to experience the American life and culture. The person in charge of our living and learning is called Jonathan Morrell, Dean of Enrollment Management. His meticulous care moved me to tears over and over again; therefore, we all affectionately called him "Grandpa." He would ask the cooks in the canteen to prepare spicy food especially for us children from the earthquake-stricken area. He would choose winter clothes for every kid in person. He would accompany us to take the tests. He would praise in the presence of others that we had made much progress. Once, I asked Grandpa why he was so kind to us kids who were actually strangers to him. He answered that we were not strangers any more and that we were his pride, his children. Yes! No matter how large the world is, strangers may become intimate friends as long as there is love. Every time we received care and love from Grandpa and from the other teachers in the college, we wished that we would pass them on and on.

When we parted, Grandpa and Grandma waved goodbye to us outside the bus window. Grandpa said he would go to China, and we told him that we would come back again. It is true that we can treat the American "Grandparents" as our own family even though we have different skin colors, nationalities and cultures. I still remember that my primary school teachers taught us to say the school motto: We should be proud of ourselves as Chinese. We take pride in our country not only because she has a long history but also because she will have a splendid and promising future. I hope that my American Grandparents can also see what the Chinese future will be. I know that I shoulder the responsibilities that my folks and American friends have entrusted me. We should act as links between the two cultures so that friendship can be established between the people in the two countries and more people can get to know and hence love China.

We will not only extend our gratitude to our American friends, but also undertake the tasks our motherland has given us. The government officials took much care of us. On April 13, a State Councilor called Liu Yandong came to see us. When I, on behalf of all the Chinese students in Cobleskill, told her that we would, like her, work for our motherland with our strong body for fifty years, I saw her eyes filled with tears. She took my hands, telling us that our motherland and people were taking care of us and supporting us. At the moment, I felt fully moved, feeling that a powerful motherland is behind us, backing us up. Peng Keyu, Consul General, made a special trip from New York to visit us. He listened to

our stories, and constantly told us, like a dear uncle, to keep safe and healthy. Tu Wentao, Director-General of the Education Department of Sichuan Province, also made a special trip here to visit us from Chengdu. Greeting us in Sichuan dialect, he gave us much inspiration.

With Director-General Tu Wentao of the Education Department of Sichuan Province

When we got off from the plane, seeing the intimate smiles from the aunts and uncles from China Scholarship Council (CSC) and receiving their embrace, we knew that we came back to our motherland. In the very situation of H1N1 flu spreading, none of them wore masks or protective suits, and we were much moved by it. Though we were isolated for the observation of possible H1N1 case, without seeing our parents and friends we had missed so long, we had much comfort with the aunts and uncles' company. Intimate smiles and warm words indicate that their care and greeting were given not only to us 150 university students but also our family and folks in our earthquake-stricken hometown. We know that we should convert the warmth into the resolution of our hometown reconstruction and courage to face any difficulty.

We have learned to be grateful and realized the responsibility we bear, and we have also got lots of friendship and care. We will strive and pursue our dream together. We departed from our motherland, and walked onto the stage of the world. Our one-year experience in the United States has enabled us to build up confidence and determination in creating more moving deeds and miracles. At the time of saying goodbye, we all held our certificates, tossed the caps printed "I love NY" at the same time, and sang together a farewell song at the Consulate-General of the P. R. C. in New York. We are a group of happy kids!

The kids of the CSC-SUNY 150 Program went to New York from Chengdu, to the United States from China, hand in hand, shoulder by shoulder. We will, in the same way, support one another and strive together, conveying love and wish, and reconstructing our hometown. We believe, our hometown will have a promising future!

Dreaming the future, aiming the world.

Tang Ji, from Deyang City, Sichuan Province.

I study Finance at Southwestern University of Finance and Economics. During my nine months in the US, I studied at SUNY − Cobleskill.

CSC-SUNY 150 Program in My Mind's Eye

By Zeng Yiming
Southwestern University of Finance and Economics

In mid July, 2008, I received a notice of nomination for the CSC-SUNY 150 Program. At that very moment, I was in the heavily-stricken earthquake area, Mianzhu, engaged with my teammates in the post-earthquake research named "Supplying Farmers with Scientific Knowledge." Consecutive hot days delayed our progress. It was worrisome that the situation in the temporary settlements was not good. More often than not, our tears were mingled with sweat in our efforts to help people in the earthquake area!

At the beginning, I took the opportunity lightly because the competition was fierce and because the research was so significant that I was unwilling to give it up. After a series of selections, I was lucky to be chosen as one of the 150 Chinese students from the earthquake-stricken area to go to the United States. At that time, my feeling was rather complex, with both joy and a feeling of being guilty. Actually I felt more guilty than joyful because I had to give my research up, without realizing my ideal of doing something for the country people in the earthquake-stricken area; therefore, I felt sorry because my teammates were still persistent in the research. If I went to the United States, I would live an easy life, with much care and love from all walks of life, while my folks were still suffering from what the earthquake had left them.

With such contradictory feelings, we 150 students left for the United States to further our study overseas.

Time flies. When I recall my days spent in SUNY − Cobleskill, they are still fresh in my mind.

In the past year in the United States, I achieved a lot. I learned what I had no chance to get, got many people's heartfelt care and love, went to many places I dreamed about, and participated in many significant activities. I believe all of these will be valuable assets in my lifetime and solid foundations in my pursuit of my dreams.

And I've got far move than these!

As a university student of journalism, I remind myself at times that I should observe things at a higher level. In my pursuit of study in the United States for nine months, I never forgot my mission as a journalist. I recorded every aspect of the CSC-SUNY 150 Program, reflecting from the perspective of a journalist on the significance behind the program—a historical stroke of Sino-American cultural exchange.

A century ago, the overseas Chinese students came back to their motherland and became celebrities in the political, military and commercial worlds, and technical backbones of factories, railroads, mines and construction industry. They were active in every field in the contemporary society, and made tremendous contributions.

Nowadays, the CSC-SUNY 150 Program is far more significant than that!

The program provided the 150 students from the earthquake-stricken area with the opportunity to study in the United States for one year, aiming at cultivating a young group to become talents in both their expertise and excellent leadership.

The 150 Chinese students went to twenty-two campuses of the State University of New York to receive their education in accordance with their majors at home, including finance, economics, agriculture, environment, information, biology, chemistry, construction, electronics, medical science, English, and Teaching Chinese as a Second Language, etc.

In the past nine months, we have been so grateful to those who have helped us, borne in mind the mission granted us, and studied hard overcoming the language barriers and taking no notice of fatigue and hardship. Consequently, we have achieved very good results, and

received much appreciation from teachers and students on the campuses.

In January, 2009, the State University of New York held Leadership Training Program in Washington and Clinton respectively. In the one-week training, the university gave us a concentrated leadership training by means of lectures, seminars and community services.

We learned a lot in the training, and accordingly our ability of leadership was largely improved. Moreover, our excellent performances in the activities brought joy to our American teachers.

Golden opportunities and unremitting efforts mean the dawn of success. We have every reason to believe that we are excellent enough to carry on our motherland's modernization construction, making accomplishments in our own fields and contributing to our hometown reconstruction.

Besides, the 150 Chinese students have another identity—conveyors of the Chinese culture.

There is an increasing intimacy for the Sino-American culture exchange to enhance the mutual understanding of the two peoples. But the fact is that, when we were in the United States, we found how limited the Americans' understanding of China is! There are even misunderstandings about the eastern giant. All these may result from the historical accumulation, and can be settled by the joint efforts of both parties.

The appearance of the CSC-SUNY 150 Program served as an effective channel to enhance the mutual understanding between the two countries. The 150 Chinese students acted as culture conveyors, publicizing the Chinese culture to Americans, answering their questions, and getting to know the American culture before taking it back to our country. We completed our tasks and made great contributions.

We were enthusiastic, confident and modest, setting up an outstanding image as Chinese university students. We were ready to help others by taking part in the public welfare activities in the communities, and were popular with the local people. We organized the Chinese Culture Show, teaching Americans Chinese and calligraphy, and in these ways tried our best to publicize the Chinese culture. We were patient in answering the questions our American friends posed, courageously defending our country's sovereignty as to some sensitive issues raised in class.

Our endeavor achieved more returns than expected.

The overseas mainstream media competed in reporting our activities, which made more and more people begin to attach importance to China. The American students respected us, loved us and had more understanding about China. Under our influence, more and more people took interest in the Chinese culture, embarking on their Chinese learning. Many American families took us as their family members, proudly telling their friends about the Chinese children staying at their homes and the children's strong motherland—China.

With the acceleration of globalization, the 150 students from the program, as culture conveyors between the two giant countries, are bound to play a more positive role in the future Sino-American communication and cooperation in various fields.

Love never fails.

Zeng Yiming, from Dujiangyan City, Sichuan Province.

I study Finance and Economic News at Southwestern University of Finance and Economics. During my nine months in the US, I studied at SUNY – Cobleskill.

My Travel to the United States

By Wang Jiao
Sichuan Agricultural University

Now it is 3:44 p. m., May 24, 2009, local eastern standard time in America. At this very moment I am on the plane flying from New Jersey to Beijing. The plane has been flying for nearly three hours, and the other passengers are asleep. Nine months ago, we 150 Chinese students from the earthquake-stricken area boarded the plane from Beijing to the John F. Kennedy International Airport of the United States. Three months after the earthquake, we, with our dreams, got to twenty-two campuses of the State University of New York to pursue our nine-month study. SUNY – Cobleskill, where I studied is only forty minutes' drive from Albany, the capital city of New York State. It is a university focusing on

With my dear classmates in the classroom

agriculture, and having what a university should own though there are not many students and the campus is relatively small. Small as the Cobleskill Campus is, we learned a lot there in the nine months. The time spent there was rather long because we missed our family, and also quite short because we felt we still had much to learn.

During our study in the United States, the leaders, teachers, friends and classmates gave us every possible care, which really moved us a lot. After the devastating May 12 Wenchuan Earthquake had happened, the State University of New York (SUNY) and our government made joint efforts to carry out the CSC-SUNY 150 Program. Within one month, we 150 students from the earthquake-hit area were quickly selected and left for the United States. Just upon our arrival in New York, we were warmly welcomed by the overseas Chinese, and the employees in the Consulate-General. When we got to our campuses, the teachers and students helped us enthusiastically. Liu Yandong, the State Councilor, and several leaders from the Ministry of Education made a special trip to visit and greet us during their stay in the United States. The governor of New York State invited us to plant trees in his residence. Peng Keyu, Consul General, specifically went to the campuses to see us and enquire about our life and study overseas. For the reason that we were studying in SUNY, the head of SUNY − Cobleskill specially went to Sichuan Agricultural University during his visit to China in April this year, and successfully signed some contractual programs …. Love was everywhere around us, and our gratitude in our mind is beyond description.

Speaking of gratitude, I have to mention Jonathan and Trudy. Jonathan, a lovely elderly man in his sixties took care of life and study of us eighteen children at Cobleskill. He was an enthusiastic and kind-hearted elderly man, so we all called him "Grandpa." The addressing of him was well-known among us all. Trudy, his partner who had the same temperament as Grandpa's,

On May 15, 2009, visiting our dear Grandpa

loved to give everybody of us a hug, so we called her "Grandma". They were like our parents during our stay in the United States.

We would share our happiness and sorrow with our American Grandparents, like the wonderful Florida trip or Boston travel. A very close relationship between Grandparents and us was thus established. Just upon our arrival at Cobleskill, in order to let us quickly get accustomed to the university life, Grandpa would come to the canteen to have meals and talks with us. Grandpa and Grandma celebrated their birthdays on the same day. They felt so happy because we eighteen Chinese students had a big meal in a Chinese restaurant with them, and gave them specially-prepared typical Chinese presents. After dinner, Grandpa began to count the number of the students attending the birthday party, and got ready to go back home. We still remember what Grandpa said before he went back home, "I will keep counting like this until you leave America. " Every touching moment made mutual love deeper. Grandparents told us that they would come to China to see us, send us the pictures of the Chinese roses planted on the "May 12" anniversary, and remember the lovely Chinese students forever.

Nine months elapsed quickly. We learned to grow up and communicate with the American students. All of us were more self-confident and became mature physically and mentally. In the two semesters, we were really busy! On the day before we departed, the Chinese aunts and uncles there invited us to a farewell dinner, and then the Consulate-General of the P. R. C. in New York arranged us a farewell party, too. All of us 150 students and all those who had cared and helped us sang karaoke songs in the consulate. We sang and sang, and felt so happy that we hugged one another and kept sobbing, singing the famous Chinese song "Friends. " At this moment something was deeply engraved in our minds, blessings from kind people who are like family members, care and love from brothers and sisters, farewell of friends. Our kind-hearted American friends, thank you all for your help! Because of what you have done to us, our new life will begin; because of you, our fate will get changed; because of you, we have learned to grow up and face new challenges courageously. The moment the plane took off, I clearly knew that we had to say goodbye. Goodbye, my dear teachers! Goodbye, my dear American classmates! Goodbye, America! I believe there will be a day when we may meet each other again, and that day won't be far away!

I think I'm more confident and brave. My best wishes to those who helped us!

Wang Jiao, from Chongzhou City, Sichuan Province.

I study Biotechnology at Sichuan Agricultural University. In America, I studied at SUNY – Cobleskill. My hobbies are reading, jogging and playing badminton.

A Brief Note of the Journey to the United States

By Yu Haitao

Southwestern University of Finance and Economics

When I was waiting at Beijing Capital International Airport for the flight back to Chengdu, I then realized that I already came back to my motherland which I had been missing day and night. The nine-month life in the United States was still fresh in my mind. Tears were still lingering on my cheeks since we were so reluctant to say goodbye to our American friends, but the journey finally came to an end.

The calamity of the earthquake that took place one year ago instantly took away tens of thousands of people's lives and their property. The shadow that the earthquake cast on people's mind has not gone away completely. Living in terror and uncertainty, I spent my days until the hot July when I received an unbelievable piece of news, saying that the State University of New York (SUNY) would provide an opportunity to study in the United States for the university students from the earthquake-stricken area. Application, selection, interview and re-examination were all held in a short period of time and in a quick manner. A month later, we 150 Chinese students from Sichuan earthquake-hit area boarded the plane flying to the United States.

Cheering with my friends at Battery Park in New York City on our first arrival

Facing the brand-new environment and people in New York, I felt a bit uneasy and anxious, but more curious and excited. I can hardly forget my excitement, the wealthy city and beautiful environment when I just landed in New York. I experienced what I had not experienced before: the university campus situated at Maritime, another way of Chinese life and culture in Chinatown, and the formal interview in the Consulate-General with the heads from the university. I, a shy boy, knew that we would start a totally new life.

I, together with the other seventeen students, was assigned to study at SUNY – Cobleskill, which was located at Cobleskill, a small town with a history of two hundred years, rather in the middle of New York. After a short break, the new semester began. We studied and tried to accommodate to the new environment, and by and by we found the environment became familiar to us. Because of our "special identity," the teachers and students in the university gave us much care. A few days after I arrived at the college, I caught a cold and my nose bled. To cure my illness, RD and the doctors spent a lot of time on it. Afterwards, every time they met me, they would inquire about my health condition, and remind me that I should pay more attention to my physical health. The teachers knew that we had difficulty in following them, so they slowed down their speed of speaking and asked us from time to time if we could

follow. The employees in the canteen initiatively came up to ask us what kind of food was to our taste. They specifically prepared us Chinese students rice and noodles. Afterwards, international food was served at a chosen time every week. We were even

With Berner's family, on Thanksgiving Day

invited to participate in making the menu for ourselves. Sometimes we were provided cooking facilities to cook for ourselves. With so many people's care, we could live comfortably and warmly. By and by, we felt at ease with the teaching methods of the American teachers, were able to follow their pace of teaching, and improved our English rapidly. What's more, we had more communication with the students around us and made lots of friends of our age. After class, we actively participated in various activities organized by the college.

With Grandpa Jonathan at Harvard University

Over 200 days and nights is a short time in our life span; however, there were so many moving stories for us to recollect in our later years of life. We give our gratitude to those who have helped and cared us. Numerous people, including government officials and ordinary employees, made tremendous efforts to the program. It was their hard work that enabled me to have such a valuable chance to study in the United States after the anguishing earthquake had happened and to get so much help from people here, among whom Jonathan Morrell, a teacher at Cobleskill, was a representative. This kind-hearted Grandpa began to care us in every aspect as soon as we arrived at the campus. When he got to know that some of us had no computers, Grandpa contacted the salesclerks and took us to buy one. Worrying that we could not tolerate the freezing winter in New York, he applied for some budgets and bought each of us warm clothes and boots. On holidays, he invited us to his home to have dinner and see movies, and took us to travel, trying his utmost to help us save money. Every other week he would let us hold a meeting to get to know how we were getting along, carefully take notes of our demands and desires and do his best to satisfy us. The most unforgettable was that he had formed the habit of counting the number of the Chinese students, "One, two... seventeen, eighteen!" Obviously, we were already his eighteen children in his mind. On the farewell morning, when we heard the familiar counting voice, tears kept running down our cheeks...

Grandpa was one of those who helped and cared us. Behind us hundreds of people did something for us and numerous people in our motherland backed us up. The earthquake calamity could take away people's lives, but wish and love remained. We said goodbye to those who had helped us, but our gratitude would be entrenched in our mind. Love will be passed on and on, and the spirit of the CSC-SUNY 150 Program will never end!

With Dr. Zingale after the graduation ceremony

Ask not what the world can do for you, ask what you can do for the world.

Yu Haitao, from Mianyang City, Sichuan Province.

I study Finance at Southwestern University of Finance and Economics. From 2008 to 2009, I studied at SUNY - Cobleskill. I'm a boy of integrity and honesty. I love reading, watching movies, and playing ball games. I hope to devote myself to the well-being of the society.

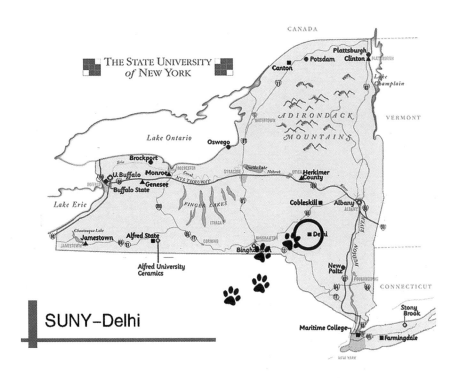

THE STATE UNIVERSITY
of NEW YORK

SUNY–Delhi

Recollections of My Life on an American Campus

By Jiang Lihui
Southwest Jiaotong University

I want to record the nine-month life in the United States in detail, but it is hard since there are so many stories to tell. When I recall the past months, maple leaves on the campus appear afresh in my memory. Therefore, I decide to entitle my essay "Recollections of My Life on an American Campus."

We 150 Chinese students from the earthquake-stricken area were assigned to twenty-two campuses of the State University of New York (SUNY). The campus on which I studied is located on the beautiful Catskill Mountain in Delhi. Last August we

With my friend in front of the gate of SUNY – Delhi

came to the Delhi Campus of SUNY. It was autumn at that time, so in my view were maple trees all over the mountain, dark green trees and azure sky. I, with some worries, expected and longed for my unknown future life. Anyway, my new life began quietly here, like a picture being unfolded slowly in front of me.

In September our class began. I had butterflies in my stomach when I took my first class because I did not know whether it was a challenge to me. After all, I had to face it, so I opened my textbook and listened to the teacher, learning and thinking as the teacher had required. At the end of the first day, I felt fairly easy. However, I had difficulty in following

the teacher of American History because he spoke very fast and I was not so good at history. That afternoon, I sat under a maple tree on the meadow, thinking what I should do to catch up, with a saying popping up in my mind: Everything will be okay. The first day in the university is really unforgettable!

The days unfolded slowly in front of me in a brand-new manner. Every day I could learn lots of new things and feel the different conceptions of American education. We could communicate freely with our teachers to set forth our ideas and air our opinions. It seemed that there were no wrong answers, and therefore we didn't worry about whether or not we would make mistakes. It was especially true in my Novel Appreciation class! For this subject, we would read a novel or short story every two days, and then write our comments on it. Our teachers would also comment on our assignments after reading them. The next time there would be a seminar at which we could talk about the author, characters or the things and people related to us. What we always heard were our teachers' praises and encouragements, which I think is the prominent characteristic of American education. Although every teacher teaches in his or her own way, it's not hard for students to follow. In class, we were also able to learn from other classmates' modes of thinking and their values as to how to deal with things and life, which could only be learned in our class communication. With regard to learning in the United States, the features lie in independent thinking, creativity, communication and cooperation.

When I could accommodate myself to the study and life there gradually, maple leaves began to change their colors from original green to red, yellow, orange and then light green...

In the nine-month stay in the United States, we traveled to many places like Los Angeles and San Francisco in California. It is really beautiful there, with very fine weather and various sorts of plants which could be found in the frigid zone and tropical zone. The cities are very lovely, with many buildings like the ones in cartoons and shops decorated in colorful letters. We also went to Harvard University and Massachusetts Institute of

Technology, two top universities in the world which many students are longing for. We could not enter the library of Harvard University because we had no student cards. Nonetheless, the academic atmosphere was rigorous enough for us to worship. It was wintertime when we got there, the whole campus was covered with heavy snow. Seeing the diligent students go into and out of the library and classrooms, I was fully respectful of them.

Actually, it was windy and snowy most of the time during our stay in the United States. The snowy season lasted for nearly six months from October 2008 to April 2009. In such cold weather we spent our Halloween, Thanksgiving Day, joyful Christmas, and Easter. Among the many interesting American holidays, I liked Christmas best. The gifts hanging on the Christmas trees were so beautiful and amazing; in the legend lovely deer were running at night pulling the sleigh on which sat mysterious Santa Clause; and the lit hearth added a tinge of romance to the holiday.

My time in the United States was neither long nor short. Snow began to melt and maple trees budded, signifying that another spring came back and that it would not be long for us to go back to our motherland. Occasionally, in the morning when birds were chirping and in the evening when the moon was shining, I would ask myself what I had learnt and gained in the past year. For many times I thought of the article I learned in my junior high school entitled "My Experience at the Age of Thirteen," a story about how Tian Xiaofei, a Chinese student, passed the entrance exam to Beijing University at the age of thirteen and lived a university life. In that article, there was such a line, "When asked about the two years' 'gain' or 'loss' at university, I could hardly use the two words to measure the well-spent time full of sweat, tear and laughter." All of a sudden I felt that this was a real feeling. I could not tell what I had gained or lost, either. Perhaps a person is bound to gain or lose something in his life, which can be eventually concluded as growth.

Under the quiet maple trees, I recalled my experiences one by one, which resembled a bunch of beads shining in the river of my life. In those days, I not only stayed with my classmates, but also made many friends there.

Uncle Bernie and Aunt Kathy are the two people who moved me a lot. During my stay in the United States, it was they who encouraged me and helped me take care of myself. This experience made me aware of the fact that I was no longer a young child. After class, I did a part-time job as well. I worked at the café in the university library, taking orders, and baking donuts or making coffee. From the part-time job, I learned that doing a job well is not easy. Overall speaking, there were hard times and happy moments.

When maple leaves became dark green, it was time for me to go back to China. I was on tenterhooks, the same feeling as what I had when I just arrived here. I asked myself again and again, "What if I have another chance to come to the United States?" The answer was the same every

My best friend Uncle Bernie

time, "I will live the same life as I have led in America." I still remember the situation when I just arrived at the university. I was not used to the life there, and missed my family, teachers, classmates and friends. But as time went by, everything changed for the better. Excitement, worry, unhappiness and curiosity were all gone. Instead, I became calm and got accustomed to the American life.

My recollections, happy or unhappy, would be deeply rooted in my mind. The days spent right after I arrived are still vivid in my eyes: my lonely figure on the meadow after the first American History class, the happy feeling I had when I completed all the writing tasks and was asked to leave earlier, my walking on the snowy ground with my roommate Yang

Ke after class, and my feeling at a loss when given the exam questions I had no time to prepare for. All this, regret or gain, will be remembered forever as a valuable asset in my lifetime. The period of my stay in the United States was also the time when I experienced the most complicated and contradictory feelings—joy, excitement, sadness, coldness, missing and surprise. I saw many things that I had never thought of, and met many people that I had had no chance to meet—exotic sceneries, different local customs and practices, bustling metropolitan cities, tranquil villages, amiable teachers, lovely classmates, warm-hearted and intimate friends. The world is subtle and relatively small because we have got to know so many people and experienced so much. The world is also comparatively large and mysterious because there is always something that waits for our exploration and discovery.

Part of our beautiful memories—a maple tree on SUNY – Delhi Campus

At the time of departure, maple leaves all over the campus were still green, which could be taken as the background for our American travel, reflecting our unforgettable experiences which were engraved deeply or shallowly on the "shell of memory."

Every time the "memory tide" rises, the "shell" will lightly touch my feet, and then ebbs slowly. My experiences are just like the vast, joyful and serene sea. I hope that I can know how to keep cherishing my valuable experiences and can sing happily on my future journey. What the past year gave us are unceasing valuable experiences.

During our studies in SUNY - Delhi, we grew up. And in this CSC -SUNY 150 Program, we got a lot of care and help from others; we will do our best and pass on the love.

Jiang Lihui, from Mianyang City, Sichuan Province.

I study in School of Foreign Languages of Southwest Jiaotong University. During my nine months in the US, I studied at SUNY − Delhi.

My Life in the United States

By Ma Jiehao
Southwest University of Science and Technology

When I, as a Chinese student from the CSC-SUNY 150 Program, recall my nine-month study and life in the United States, there are as many things as stars in the sky, which deserve recollecting and pondering. Needless to say, I have gained a lot from the American classes and my contemplations. What I would like to share with my friends most is my experience of the American life and culture.

The first impression the United States gave me is its wonderful environment. Even in New York, the most prosperous city in the world, the sky is azure blue. The campus of the State University of New York where I studied is situated at the Catskill Mountain; the scenery there is more than picturesque. The slope, woods, endless grassland, and closely-planted corn fields are so beautiful! The summer green and the autumn blazing colors always gave me good moods. The sky is so blue that planes usually leave wonderful traces when flying by. Various kinds of wildlife live freely on this land. It is not strange to see crows flying overhead, squirrels jumping on the campus trees, and wild turkeys walking on the roadside or in the fields. It was a big

A view of SUNY – Delhi

surprise for us to see four wild deer behind our dormitory.

Americans live comfortably because they have a beautiful natural environment and every small part of the surrounding is people-oriented. On the university campuses, in tourist attractions, shopping centers and even on the roadsides drinking-water machines can easily be found to satisfy people's need. Along every corridor inside the dormitories, there are lighted signs for people's escape in time of emergency. In every room there is a most sensitive fire alarm system, monitoring around the clock the concentration of smoke. One day, a girl in our room forgot to turn on the smoke-exhaust ventilator when cooking. The cooking smoke triggered the fire alarm. Consequently, all the students ran out of the building and the campus policemen arrived at the scene within five minutes. It sounds exaggerated, but it shows that Americans have a strong consciousness of safety. To Americans, personal security guarantee is the first and foremost thing to consider. Another thing that has touched me particularly is that the disabled in the United States are well taken care of in their daily life. In many buildings there are sets of barrier-free access, and specifically designed slopes, toilets and hand-washing basins for them. On our Delhi Campus there is no lack of such facilities. I often saw on the campus that quite a few disabled students went into and out of the teaching buildings and canteens in wheelchairs. With the special facilities, together with their fellow students' voluntary help, the disabled could enjoy university life freely.

Of course, the intriguing parts of life are not only embodied in the scenery and facilities, but also in people. I was always moved by the friendship given to me by my American teacher's and classmates. They not only offered us various kinds of help at the university, but also invited us to their homes on conventional American holidays. On Halloween, we were invited to our good friend Amy's home to carve pumpkin lanterns, watching weirdly-dressed kids carry their pails and ask for candy from door to door. On Thanksgiving Day, we ate a big turkey dinner at the teacher's home. Although there was a heavy snow outside the window, the warm gentle candle light on the table gave me a feeling of cozy home. At Christmas, we played with a group of lovely kids at the president's home, listening to stories about Santa Claus, and we also got our gifts under the Christmas tree. Every time we had a very good time. Celebrating various conventional western holidays in American families is another way of experiencing the American culture.

In America university students enjoy many holidays. Besides being invited to American families, we also make good use of the holiday time to make package tours. We visited many tourist attractions in famous American cities, such as the roof of the Empire State Building and the Times Square in New York, campuses of Harvard University and Massachusetts Institute of Technology in Boston, Walt Disney World Resort in Orlando, Florida, the Frank Lloyd Wright Home and Studio in Chicago, the Sunset

Making Jack-o'-Lantern in Amy's home on Halloween

Boulevard in Los Angeles, and the Golden Gate Bridge in San Francisco. These travels enriched my knowledge about American politics, economy and culture. As a student of architecture, I think there is nothing more interesting than visiting those famous buildings that I saw in my textbooks time and time again. I was lucky to be able to appreciate in person the villas and skyscrapers designed by the famous architects, and I gained a lot from each travel.

Besides the famous buildings, what also made me linger were various kinds of museums in major American cities, concerning art, history, astronomy, and biology. Lots and lots of invaluable works of art can be seen in these museums which are open for people to visit at very low price or free of charge. To me, these museums are an embodiment of the cultural atmosphere in major cities and their impacts on the public are immeasurable.

Christmas Eve at the house of the president of SUNY – Delhi

The nine-month stay in the United States was so short a time, but the recollections are so abundant! During the period, I attempted to contemplate and integrate into the new land with an open and tolerant mind. While I broadened my view, I would like to compare what I saw and heard in America with those of my hometown and my country. The differences between the United States and China cannot be evaluated as right or wrong. However, the process of comparing the phenomena and contemplating things made me more mature to view the world. In my mind, what I saw, felt and contemplated is more precious than what I learned from the American classes. I am lucky that I was able to have the opportunity to study in the United States at the age of twenty so that I could get to know how large and wonderful the world is. My nine-month stay in the United States, though short, is very significant for my growth!

Experiences build up life.

Ma Jiehao, from Pengzhou City, Sichuan Province.

I study Architecture at Southwest University of Science and Technology. In America, I studied at SUNY – Delhi. I'm a very sunny girl. The habit of drawing led me to the architecture major and then made me love it more than I thought. Though I'm not the most outstanding person among all people of my age, I have strong confidence in myself. I would always try my best.

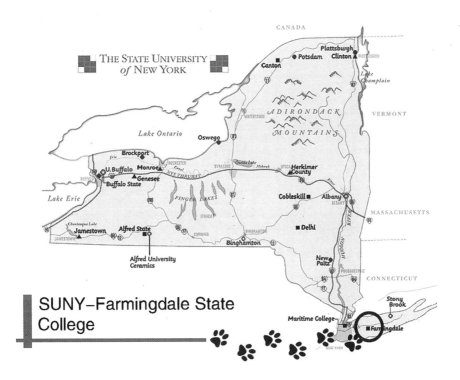

THE STATE UNIVERSITY *of* NEW YORK

SUNY–Farmingdale State College

An Unforgettable Experience

By Mu Zijian
Sichuan University

"You're my favorite student, " my favorite teacher, Robert Reganse, Professor of Economics said to me when he granted his cherished pen to me on the graduation ceremony. This experienced professor, who gained his popularity among students with his sense of humor, also told me that during his thirty years of Macro and Micro Economics' teaching, he had witnessed several presidential elections and repeated the jokes nearly every year, but among the numerous students he had taught in the past thirty years he told me his favorite student is—"It is you, Mu. " He loved my loads of Chinese history stories, enjoyed my discussion with him on financial crisis and financial tsunami after classes, and appreciated my leading position in the class. What surprised him most is that the nineteen Chinese students to Farmingdale from the earthquake-hit area were not sad, depressed and passively waiting for cares and sympathy as he had imagined. On the contrary, each of us was optimistic, sunny, caring others and actively promoted Chinese culture in a foreign country. He said he was proud of us for this. We are proud of ourselves, too.

Over the past one year, many of the Chinese families in New York and teachers in school have taken every effort to help us live happily here. They tried to give us busy schedules every weekend so that we might not feel lonely. They invited us to go to beaches, enjoy the sunshine, go hiking in mountainous areas, have Sichuan meals in their places (the twice-cooked meat was always the dish to be finished first), eat hotpot, play volleyball, go skiing, go skating, visit the music hut, visit the botanical garden, the zoo, the museum and Broadway.... We did have a fruitful and wonderful year.

But we knew well that we were not there to travel. We gained a lot and achieved a lot. The more important thing is we learned to offer, to display and to strive hard. We didn't forget the responsibility and expectation we shouldered. Apart from study (We achieved A nearly in every course, which surprised our professors and classmates), we also shouldered the responsibilities of enhancing Sino-American relationship. We applied to be volunteers in the activity of raising money for Polar Bear Plunge for Special Olympics in New York; and we, the students from Sichuan, undertook all the volunteering and coordinating work in 2009 Asian-American Culture Festival of Long Island. On Dec. 10, 2008, we nineteen students held a vivid Chinese Culture Show. With the help of staff members from the Consulate-General of the P. R. C. in New York (who generously offered traditional Chinese costumes in various dynasties), we planned and played five performances—Chinese etiquette, Chinese costume, Chinese dishes(especially Sichuan dishes), Chinese calligraphy, and Chinese dancing. The auditorium was full of audience with corridors full of people, and some came with their babies in their baby- trolleys. One of the teachers used five different words to praise our performance. He said this was the most exciting show he had had at school where he had been teaching for twenty-six years.

Thanks to Mom Kathy, Farmingdale Campus became the most active school in the CSC-SUNY 150 Program. Kathy was actually responsible for media business at school, and she did not have to care for us

In February 2009, Princeton University, poem citation "Thankful for Love"

nineteen students from Sichuan. But the first moment she met us, she began to take us as her own kids. Every one of us would get a mysterious gift from her at his/her birthday. Two buses would take nineteen of us to her place on every single holiday, to enjoy talks and meals. We were short of costumes and stage props for holding the Chinese Culture Show, and she drove back home at once to pick her mom's dress and her own bowls and tea-pots for our performance. I was asked for several times the question "When did you get the most help from Kathy?" Well, it is too hard to answer this question. She is just like our mother. Every time we had problems, it was Kathy whom we would go for help. She has never complaint about our bothers. She is the loveliest person in my eyes. She encouraged me to be a leader, to try any new and wonderful things. Everybody has a dream of America, and my dream of America is great because of Kathy.

I have a Chinese dream as well. I saw Premier Wen Jiabao as a representative of the 150 college students from the earthquake-hit area when he met the overseas Chinese representatives during his trip to U. N. on September 24, 2008. When interviewed by the local Chinese media upon the question about whether he had any words for the 150 students on the CSC-SUNY 150 Program, our Premier said, "I miss them so much. Each time on my visit to Beichuan, I was deeply moved by the people there each time. I know the students also miss me from their letters. Please give my regards to them. I hope they will become strong and brave. I hope they can make some achievements some day. And I hope they have their hometown and motherland in heart." I saw tears in his eyes when he said these words. Premier Wen has visited Beichuan for seven times in the short time after the earthquake and I know he loves there as much as I do. My Chinese dream is in Beichuan. I hope people in my hometown will get rid of the nightmare and face the life optimistically. I hope they will be strong and brave people with achievements as the premier expects.

On January 26, 2009, the Chinese New Year's Day, twenty representatives of us met Yao Ming in New York in the NBA Cares Activity. Yao Ming's Yao Foundation would invest to establish five Hope

Schools in Sichuan. We eagerly offered our suggestions. I suggested to Yao that as a Qiang Nationality in Beichuan, I realized that the Qiang culture was dying out. The Qiang language is especially at a critical point. Language is the blood of a culture and Qiang culture can not survive without its language. On behalf of this minority nationality, I hope Bilingual Teaching of Putonghua and Qiang Language could be carried out in the Hope School so that Qiang history could be preserved and Qiang culture could be enhanced. Yao Ming said it was the first time for him to hear about such a situation and he was aware of the significance of language and culture to China. He said he would take this matter into serious consideration. My classmates also suggested that with the 150 students on CSC-SUNY 150 Program, more university students from the earthquake-hit area be volunteers in the schools supported by Yao Ming. Yao Ming listened to us carefully and said that he was amazed at our marvelous ideas.

January 27, 2009, New York, interviewed by *New York Times* Columnist George Vesey before the meeting with Yao Ming

He said we are, as he is, the bridge between China and the rest of the world, and we will be able to change the world in the future. We took Yao as our friend instead of a star and we took this chance to discuss about the plan to make the earthquake-hit area better. We are proud of ourselves.

I met the ex-vice president of SUNY, Mr. Denis Simon, on the ceremony on which State Councilor Liu Yandong was conferred with an Honorary Doctor of Laws by Stony Brook University. Mr. Denis Simon speaks good Chinese. He did a lot for the CSC-SUNY 150 Program. Before we started for the States in 2008, in his speech given at Sichuan University he threw a wet blanket on us, who were looking forward to the visit to the States, by telling us that "It is not easy to study in the States because you'll have to update yourselves everyday so as not to get lost. The standard to check your everyday progress is Knowledge + Friends + Fun." I exactly followed his suggestion and I was very happy to meet him again. I told him how excellent we were in the exams and how many international friends we had made. What was especially meaningful was many of us realized our responsibility and were eager to go back to our hometown to help in various ways, such as teaching English. I thought he would be happy with our ideas and give us some encouragement. But out of my expectation, he threw a wet blanket on me again. He said it was good to have a sense of responsibility and passion for hometown, but ideas were crucial. "A good idea will help one get twice the result with half the effort, while an immature idea may ruin a good deed." What he mentioned was to help the reconstruction of our hometown. He was right. Scientific and innovative ideas are badly needed back home. We should do more than merely joining the reconstruction. We should do it creatively. What is the meaning of CSC-SUNY 150 Program? We were not sent to the States merely to broaden our horizon. We are the future leaders of the earthquake-hit area and the innovation and revolution we are going to bring there should be unduplicated, and innovation and revolution will come from our observation, thoughts and communication. For me, each of these 150 students has a bright future. CSC-SUNY 150 Program is just like a taking-off airplane whose power inspires us to associate it with decisive opportunities of change and makes us imagine that some day in the future we will be climbing and reaching a new height.

One hundred years ago, Boxer Indemnity opened a gate for Chinese people to go and study abroad on a large scale. Studying abroad cultivated Mei Yiqi, the ex-president of Qinghua University, Hu Shi, the Chinese Literature Master, Zhu Kezhen, the meteorologist, to name but a few. One hundred years later, we are somewhat similar to those precursors with the difference that we are from the earthquake-hit area. I believe some of us will become pillars of these areas or even of the country.

The past one year was a special one in my life and my fate will be

changed because of it. I learned how to share and how to love in this year. Something has been left there in the States, some has accompanied me back home, and some will stay in my memory forever.

You never know until you try.

Mu Zijian, a Qiang Nationality from Beichuan County, Sichuan Province.

I'm from Wu Yuzhang College (Honors College) in Sichuan University. As a student representative, I was received by Premier Wen Jiabao, and I was a student in charge of many programs and activities in CSC-SUNY 150 Program.

Do You Have a Yankee Stadium in Your Heart?
—To Record My Simple but Wonderful Time in the States

By Wang Sidi
Southwest Jiaotong University

I still remember my simple but wonderful time across the Pacific Ocean up to now and will keep it in my memory for ever.

When I was in Long Island in New York I had a complicated feeling when I heard that we were going to leave for home: I was eager to place a bunch of white roses at the place where my father forever rests his active heart; I felt sorry for my mom because I got so much here but left her dealing with the cruel after-quake difficulties by herself; and I owed my best friends and teachers a big hug for their companions and encouragement and I could not wait to rush back home to do so.

All the things that took place in the past 365 days made me feel, though still in sorrow, that what had happened in this year was just like a butterfly that had laid loads of "memory eggs" from which my strength and happiness were bred. This strength and happiness would last for the rest of my life.

In New York, I found in the Yankee Stadium the amazing happiness and self-confidence. Though I ever wept in loneliness and felt sorry for myself, now I have become calm and determined toward life.

A Friend in Need Is a Friend Indeed

My friends there, the scenery there, the smiles there, the life there and the love there...all these gave me courage to fall asleep after weeping at night with hope for the future. "...if tomorrow never comes, I'm telling you I'm happy today, because yesterday I enjoyed a wonderful life,

and I built my 'Yankee Stadium' in my heart, to love, to fight and to show."

What a miracle! There were no barriers in spite of differences in religious belief, differences in age and title. I presented my heart and gained so much, all out of my expectation.

The team of China 150 and Ms. Wei Lin who was in charge of it gave me the most care and the sense of stability. Farmingdale 19 gave me the meaning of happiness in this year. Mr. Chen Chunyang, President of Southwest Jiaotong University, gave me a happy sense of belonging. My classmates in the States gave me the true feeling of American culture. And the new friends I made in the States—January, Mary, Mu Zijian, Sister Liu Qian from Hunan Satellite TV Station and other media at home and abroad offered me the rare chance to diong documentary and showed me with happiness and love.

Mia, a pal who accompanied me most in New York gave me the very American life that I had never expected and the happiness and strength that I needed, with which I had my own Yankee Stadium.

We, two girls at the age of twenty, both curious of foreign countries, met and started a marvelous trip because of curiosity. Mia is a typical cute American girl with wine-like red hair and drives a lovely Mini Cooper. She is a party animal. She smokes and knows how to play the woman, but she is very polite. She studied in Drama School for one year. On the first registration day, I was in sound sleep when she, who looked like a Barbie to me, was taken into the dorm by RA. I got to know later that she had been looking forward to meeting me and had been preparing for that day for half a month when she knew that her roommate would be a Chinese girl.

We started chatting and found that we shared many common interests in music, being simple and being after free and happy life. Sharing secrets is the best way to promote friendship between girls of twenty. She told me about her romance with her boyfriend on beaches in France and Italy, and I shared with her the feeling of Chinese girls' first love to boys. We shared nearly everything. We gossiped about friends, we talked about presidential election, we had instant noodles with spices added, we had canned chips, we tried cheongsam, we tried smoked make-up, we practiced Chinese calligraphy, we went to Bowling Club every Tuesday, and we attended birthday parties together. We started to show up together.

My roommate Mia wrote down "米娅 loves Sidi," and showed to me so proudly.

She told me not long after that I looked a boring person to her the first time she saw me, but after chatting she found me nice. She said to me, "You are my best roommate ever."

I dreamed of my dad, aunty, elder sister and nephew who died in the earthquake on May 12, 2008. My crying woke Mia up. Weeping, I told her about my experience in the earthquake that night. But she opened the window and told me calmly like a big sister that she was sad to hear that, but that I should not have been so emotional. She asked me to sleep. I felt deserted at her "cold" words. However, the next day, at the cafeteria our friend Catline asked about my nightmare last night. When I was back in the dorm, I frankly told Mia that I did not want to share my sadness with others to get more affection or to make others feel sorry for me. I told her she was a lovely girl who had given me so much pleasure....

I felt extremely sad on the anniversary of the May 12 Earthquake. On that "cold" summer night, what could I do for my passed away beloved? At 2 a. m. (2 p. m. Beijing time), I asked Mia to lend me a lighter for lighting a candle. She cautiously asked me why and then asked to light one candle as well. Joined by some other friends, we went to a small gloriette outside the dormitory. At such a special moment, with the company of Mia, everyone's tears melted the ice in my heart on that early summer night in Long Land, New York.

That day, the university held a special Sino-America May 12 memorial activity for us. After the university president finished the speech, it was the turn for student representative to say something. I volunteered to share the story that had happened on me and Mia the night before. Mia came to me when the applause was over. She took off the rings on her ears and nose to show respect to such an occasion. She joined me in adding some soil to the friendship tree and had a photo with me.

I left the university with the gift from Mia. She asked me not to open until I got back. I did as told and found the gift was a piece of yellow silk on which were good wishes from twenty Farmingdale friends who started university life in 2009.

Memories with sound, quite pictures, and silent words filled my life. I felt I lost my beloved again. So long as we live earnestly, happily, and love frankly, we can have a gopher ball. Every game will come to an end, but I know she gave me a lot and I will do myself better, love better, and enjoy love better.

What Pleased Me Was a Happy Life

Keep myself busy and keep going on by forgetting the sadness—I once thought to myself.

However, my treasured friends gave me joyful tears, sunny smiles, and even crazy passion while traveling and life gave me a sense of peace and the pleasure of being stable.

I have been to the Yankee Stadium in New York, Beacon on the Long Island, Union in Chicago, Pentagon in Washington, Princeton University in New Jersey, the United States Military Academy at West Point, California State Route 1, Show Places in Las Vegas. I visited the laboratory in MIT in Boston, enjoyed hot-dogs in Philadelphia and Fire Play in Virginia. Life treated me so generously, then for what reason should I doubt about my future?

What I benefited most from the Lectures, Writing course, American History class and Economic class, Sex Psychology course and course in

Electric Major in senior grade and many other courses was to put what I had learned into practice, to absorb knowledge critically, to think logically and to present views simply.

Polar Bear Plunge for Special Olympics New York

I experienced a lot in traveling. I got embarrassed when I could not get the point while I was watching Chicago Comedy Sportz, the biggest show place for live comedy performances. Walking on the streets, I wasn't panic even if I had language problems. I am happy I have been to so many places and I am a global citizen now.

We did various kinds of volunteer work in the States—we bought flowers for friends in the event of Aids Walk New York, we raised fund in the Avon Breast Cancer Walk in New York, we handed out free brochures to enhance environmental protection awareness in communities, and we handed out leaflets on campus and promoted free checkup to prevent unnecessary abortion. What I liked most and benefited most from was to raise fund in the 28th Polar Bear Plunge, which was the largest fund raising for the running and athletes' training of the Special Olympics. I got registered on the designated website and donated $10 soon as I saw the news of fund raising. I talked with Farmingdale 19 and our American Mom Kathy about this event. The University President took the lead by donating $25 and Financial Officer at school, Richard also donated $25. More and more students joined in after I called for donations among China 150. This was something we could do to return the care to the New Yorkers for their care for us.

On the day of the Plunge, the nineteen of us started volunteer work in the communities. I bravely put on my swimming suit and dived into the freezingly cold sea water with two brave and warm hearts painted on my cheeks. I got to know later that we had raised $600 for this event through our volunteer work.

About Me Back Home

I hosted, in English, the commencement ceremony held at East River Park in New York. I presented my heartfelt gratitude and appreciation and hugged everyone to show my love and care.

Lucky as we are, we are eager to pay back what we have gained from others.

After I came back, I taught in Zhongyuan village (a small village with several hundreds of people) in Qima county in Qingchuan. I suddenly found on a quiet night that what the past year brought to me was not memory but happiness from heaven, was the attitude of being strong, optimistic, and enjoying life, was the confidence and

With my friends in Yankee Stadium

earnestness from the Star Players in the Yankee Stadium, was the belief and passion of the audience, and the traditional belief of the Yankee, "Just Win," which has helped them win twenty-six out of thirty-five professional baseball games.

What has been left when I am back? All that happened in the States has turned to be wings of dream, firm expectation and approvals in eyes. I lost a lot, but I have gained more.

Tears stay because of love, and the laughter and fears in those days have taught me something: Life is for experiencing. I learned to chase after my dreams, and to be someone stronger. It is not enough to be myself. I need to be someone stronger to help many others....

People do belong to someone, but we should get our own Yankee

Stadium. Prepare well and fight for it, beautifully.

I am taking all efforts to manage my Yankee Stadium and let it shine. How about you?

Love life, accept fate, dream about tomorrow, and seize the day.

Wang Sidi, from Mianzhu City, Sichuan Province.

I'm in Electrical Engineering Department of Southwest Jiaotong University. In America, I studied at SUNY − Farmingdale State College. As a student representative, I took an active leading part in CSC-SUNY 150 Program, greeting national leaders and hosting great performances. Meanwhile, I enthusiastically participated in various campus programs and community services with local parties.

The Youth Blossoming Abroad

By Liu Yu
Sichuan University

I

An unexpected earthquake hit Sichuan, the so-called the Heavenly Land of Plenty. Everything was ruined, and many families parted for ever.

At 2:28 p. m. on May 12, 2009, at Farmingdale State College of SUNY, nineteen university students from the earthquake-hit area planted memorial trees with their teachers and friends to memorize the dead and made good wishes for the alive.

By the blessing tree on May 12, 2009, the first Memorial Day of Sichuan Earthquake at Farmingdale State College

One year passed. We put a perfect end to our studies in the States. I still remember the last day in the States, on which our graduation ceremony was held. The 150 students of us threw the caps to the sky cheering, "I love you, New York! Goodbye, America!" America, a country that seems close but is actually far away from us. We had never thought we would have a chance to study in an American university. But, because of the earthquake in Wenchuan in 2008, State University of New

York decided to support 150 university students from the earthquake-hit area to study in the States for one year, and I was lucky to be one of them. I still remember, in the beautiful August of 2008, while the whole nation was in the glory and excitement brought by the Olympic Games, a group of university students from Sichuan, were also looking forward to their upcoming trip to the States.

Accepting honor of " Campus Ambassador " on the farewell party from the president of Farmingdale State College, May 15, 2009

On the night of August 16, 2008, we kept our eyes wide open to look around for symbols of the States when we got off the airplane at JFK International Airport. I saw the bright Strip Flag on the wall and I knew this flag would witness a Chinese university student's progress and improvement in the following nine months in the States.

II

What impressed me most in the one-year study in the States were the diversifying teaching approaches which could inspire the students' interest in studies. Take my courses in Business, Government and Society as examples. On top of giving interesting lectures, the teachers would divide us into groups to do topic reports. They sometimes invited the local officials or professors in other fields to probe into a deeper level in certain chapters. They also took us to museums which have some connection to some themes of courses to help us have a solid understanding about abstract concepts.

What come next are the well-designed and well-prepared courses. At the first meetings, teachers would brief us the content of the courses,

foundamental knowledge and tools needed for the courses as well as detailed syllabus and class management so that we could have a clear understanding of the courses we were going to take. Meanwhile we saw the wide application of Net Teaching Assisting System. Teachers would put references related to classes and updated assignments on line, and we could also submit our assignments, check our marks and contact our teachers in the same way. Forums were also provided on line for discussions.

Comprehensive assessment in courses is another important feature of university education in the States. The assessment of each course is made of five parts, including attendance, homework, program developing, quiz, and final examination. Thus, it does not work if you care only final exams. You have to try hard in every assignment; no matter it is homework or final exam. Universities in the States also paid great attention to plagiarism. Things and behaviors involve plagiarism and pirated copies and the policies and punishments on them will usually be announced on the Orientation for new students. Meanwhile, specific requirements will be given by different teachers. For example, in the course of System Analysis & Design, we needed Microsoft Office Visio and Microsoft Office Project. The teacher gave us the copyrighted number and required us to use the copyrighted ones. The teacher of Algorithm Analysis asked us to do assignment independently and told us all the plagiarism or copies from internet resources would be taken as cheating and would be reported to the school. The perfect regulation and enactment guarantee the independence in studies and the respect to the works of others.

III

The one-year stay in the States also gave me a chance to get to know the States and its culture. Let me start with NBA which is chased after by many boys. I used to think NBA was just a basketball ground with worldwide recognition, and that crazy fans, hot basketball babies and shining stadium make it a successful sports event. But after I watched several games, I found NBA also offers an opportunity and place for communications among the youths and for family activities. Team spirit, constant strivings for success, fierce competitions, and the spirit of "never giving up" have potential guidance to help the youth develop positive personalities. Also, at the beginning of each big game there would be an excellent singer leading the chorus in singing the national anthem of the United States of America. The charming and beautiful voice echoed through the whole stadium, with the quietness and courtesy of the players as a striking contrast. The sense of belonging and pride of the nation was fully displayed at that moment. For me, such a moment works better than the repeated patriotic education from the teacher. Besides, NBA also has a public charity called NBA Cares, and every player will voluntarily take part in the charity events in this program, such as building or mending houses for the poor, chatting with disabled children, playing basketball with kids on campuses and so on. I was very lucky to meet Yao Ming on the Chinese Lunar New Year's Day on behalf of the university students from the earthquake-hit area. We told him about the reconstruction of the quake-hit area and put forward some suggestions on the site-picking and planning of the primary schools which would be built with the donation from Yao Foundation.

In 2008, we also witnessed the hot and fierce competition of Presidential Election. This election, with the first African-American candidate—Barack Obama and the first female candidate for the position of vice president—Sarah Palin joining in, was doomed to be an important one in American history. The campaigns from the Republican Party and Democratic Party were carried out in the form of TV speeches, advertisements on mass medias, and propaganda on the internet. The whole nation was rapturous when Obama declared his success in election in the Grant Park. We were expecting him to make greater progress in enhancing Sino-American communication and cooperation.

I had many of my firsts in the States: On the first visit to Disneyland, which was a long cherished dream in my childhood, I cheered and applauded like a child when I saw the fireworks over the castle; on the first trip to the seaside—the magnificent Jones Beach, I was reluctant to leave when I viewed the white sand, blue sea, and flying seagulls; I got my first salary in my life and I was proud of it though it was not much; I tried Mongolian Dancing for the first time and displayed the diversified Chinese ethnic cultures to the American people; I was interviewed by the media for the first time and gave my best wishes via the camera. There are many other firsts.

With some China 150 students at Jones Beach on May 19, 2009

IV

Looking back on what happened in this past year, I have to admit that we are a group of lucky children. We have experienced exotic cultures abroad, and enjoyed wonderful life there, but we never forgot those who backed us up quietly. I would like to show my deepest gratitude to the China Scholarship Council and State University of New York for their precious scholarship, without which we could not have been abroad to receive education and experience different culture. I would also like to extend my gratitude to the Chinese in the States, from whom we got generous help and care as well as homelike warmth in a different country. My gratitude also goes to the teachers and friends in the States. Your kindness and love helped me to spend a smooth and safe study year in the States. Many more thanks stay in my heart and the only thing I could do is to pass on this love so that more people will get this very selfless love. The study in the States has come to a perfect end. We have started our new life back home and keep pursuing our dreams and targets.

The beauty of the Stars and Stripes lies in her people's passion and pride in their country rather than the banner itself.

Liu Yu, from Deyang City, Sichuan Province.

I'm a junior of College of Software Engineering in Sichuan University. I'm a Communist Party member and Vice-Party branch secretary of Grade 2006 in the college. After Wenchuan Earthquake, I volunteered to do the statistical work and data input work. Also I went back to my hometown to maintain the sanitation of temporary accommodation. As a member of China 150, I majored in Computer Engineering in SUNY – Farmingdale State College. During my year in America, I took an active part in the campus volunteer work and organized a lot of cultural activities such as Chinese Culture Show, Asian Culture Festival.

Farmingdale – Long Island – New York – the United States
—The Valuable Treasure in My Life

By He Manqiu
Sichuan University

Undoubtedly, we were lucky, going to the United States at an unusual time, and coming back to our motherland at another unusual time. What happened in the past one year was like a dream, a dream full of laughter, tears, love, and a dream from which we are reluctant to wake up. I remember well those eyes with tears at the farewell party held for us. I could not help giving a speech to reflect and appreciate the flying past one year when I was granted the Honor Certificate of Student Ambassador by the University President. I would like to share with readers this speech titled "Only Love Will Stay Forever in My Heart" to recall my beautiful overseas study trip.

Good afternoon, everyone,

It is my great honor to say a few words from the bottom of my heart on behalf of my fellow students in the China 150 in Farmingdale. I fear to face the departure. I kept telling myself to hold my tears and leave here with smile before I came up on this stage. Before I came to America, I thought nine months would be a long time for me, because that meant 274 days and nights away from my parents and friends. But now I find it too short. Departure is at the corner before I have time to reflect those good memories and fruitful experience.

My dear American mother, father, aunties, uncles, professors and friends, even an ocean's appreciation is not enough for me to show my feelings to you. Though we are not residents on this land, we are taken as part of your families, and you make us aware of international love.

If I am asked what I cherish most here in the States, I would say that is you—the lovely and respectable people. Just after the Mother's Day, our American Mom Kathy and Dad Kim held a farewell party for us at their home, and we celebrated the Mother's Day for our Mom who has the most children. I could hardly express how I felt when I left their house, how sad and reluctant I was to leave this house. I celebrated all the festivals—the Thanksgiving, Halloween and Christmas, in this house, which is full of laughter, hugs, kisses and happy talks. This is definitely our second home! It is not necessary to, nor can we, list how much Mom Kathy, as the ambassador of culture-exchanges at school, has done for us. What I want to say aloud is—I love you.

I also want to thank our most popular University President Keen. It is hard to imagine that you, as the University President, have been our driver for many times. You are a gentle and kind person. You took us to visit the museum and botanical garden in Bronx. You took us to see the largest balloon trip in Manhattan. You took us to your house and bought us the Chinese food that we had dreamed of for days and nights. We cooked hometown dishes to share with you and your cares have made us feel less homesick.

Our vice-president of university Kahn is an elegant lady. You can not imagine how busy she is everyday. But busy as she is, she always replies to our email at the fastest speed, which has touched me so much because I can feel she is always there to help and support me. I also

With some staff and Father Christmas in a skating rink in Long Island, New York on Christmas Eve, 2008

remember that shortly after my arrival in the States, I got sick because of bacteria infection and was sent to hospital by an ambulance. I was full of homesickness and frustration. But I overcame the difficulties with the cares from my friends in the States and the encouragement from the teachers and also from Kahn who helped pay the high bills. I seemed to have grown up in that experience.

Our second beloved American Mom is Lorraine, who is the dean of our

department. She has the warmest and most encouraging smile in the world. She is such a charming lady that she always gives love and hugs to people around her. I will always remember the beautiful days I spent with you, Lorraine.

My gratitude also goes to Richard, who is in charge of the financial business. We could not have had so many wonderful weekends without you, we could not have enjoyed so many movie nights accompanied by ice cream without you, and we could not have had such a deep understanding about Beetles without you. Thank you for what you have done for us.

Last but not the least, I would like to extend my gratitude to our Chinese Mom Ms. Yang. Your loving care makes my heart warm. Your red bean cake, Guihua cake and Chengdu hotpot are our treasures. You have looked after us in all aspects. Your good deeds will be rewarded, Ms. Yang, and we love you forever.

I would like to express my gratitude to many others. And I would like to thank the fate most. It is fate that helped me to meet you, to get to know you, to understand you, to love you and to be loved by you. What a happy experience!

As a member of CSC-SUNY 150 Program, I have made full use of the past nine months, and believe the other members have done the same. We have experienced things we never did in the past twenty years. In the process of understanding cultural differences, we got to learn a lot about America, about its education system, health care system, election system, traffic system, consumption styles, culture and customs, and business system, etc. We have widened our horizon by visiting New York, Washington, Boston, Florida Orlando, Disneyland, New Jersey.... Different city styles and views reflected different ideas and historical backgrounds. Harvard University, MIT, Boston University, New York University, Columbia University, Yale University, all these well-known universities have impressed us deeply. I tried to gain experience from part-time jobs, such as teaching Math, Physics, and Engineering Mechanics. I also tried to improve my English in getting along well with my coworkers and students. I worked as a guide on campus on holidays to attract more high school students to attend this university and took pictures to promote the image of our university. No matter to raise fund for Special Olympics, or to participate in the Beijing University alumni association in New York, I tried my best to do it well and I benefited a lot from such volunteer work. Experience is the most valuable treasure that could not be obtained from books. And we have grown up in these experiences....

Awarded with certificates by the president on the farewell party in May, 2009

As a team we have successfully accomplished the mission of being culture envoys between two nations. Our dearest teachers, do you remember the Chinese Culture Show the nineteen of us have presented to you? Everything of the show, from the promotion in early stage, to the program planning, costumes, rehearsal, stage effect, interaction with the audience and so on, came from us who had no experience in this aspect. We are proud of our team. Do you remember the happy time we spent in the Consulate-General, and the Leadership Training Program as well as the cleaning up activities on campus on the Earth Day? We have added some Chinese color to our campus with our effort and endeavor.

My dear friends, I would like to make a wish for all of us—I hope our friendship may grow closer, deeper and greater like the metasequoia we planted together to memorize the one year anniversary of earthquake in Wenchuan. Thank you.

Be energetic as a youth!

He Manqiu, from Mianyang City, Sichuan Province.

I study Security Engineering of Chemical Engineering Institute in Sichuan University. In America, I studied at SUNY – Farmingdale State College. When the earthquake happened, I helped transfer the relief goods and take care of the patients. In America, I took part in the organization of Asian-American Culture Festival of Long Island and the donation for paralympics.

A Bud in Blossom

By Yin Jing

Southwestern University of Finance and Economics

Ever since our departure, it has been drizzling in New York. Mother Kathy says that is God wiping away his tears and bidding us farewell, for even God is aware that people at the two ends of the bridge of love must know something well, which is, missing and worrying about each other. Yes, I miss you all. I miss you very much...

I like to call myself "the happy kid." I always feel I am a happy, lucky and merry kid, because I know I am not alone, with you behind me, with you along...

You are the ones who have stuck together through thick and thin with us; you are the ones who have fully cooperated with us, shoulder to shoulder, hand in hand. Now the severe winter has passed and spring is here again. I am sure all the buds which have weathered are bound to bloom fabulously.

Celebrating Mid-Autumn Festival with Ms. Wei Lin in Farmingdale, 2008

You are the ones who have been taking care of us like our parents. Thank you, Ms. Wei Lin (the team leader of the China 150). It is you who have accompanied us to the United States, enabling us to study and grow in a new and different world. Thank you, our dear Grandpa and aunts, Premier Wen Jiabao, State Councilor Liu Yandong, and Chen Zhili, the Vice Chairperson of the Standing Committee of the

National People's Congress. You have managed to find time among loads of work to visit us and send us the regards of our dear folks at home, which keeps reminding us of our great motherland. Thank you, Ambassador Zhou Wenzhong(Chinese Ambassador to the United States) and Consul General Peng Keyu (Consulate-General of the P. R. C. in New York). You have made us feel that even far away in America we can always find our home. Home is the Chinese Embassy in America; home is the Consulate-General of the P. R. C. in New York. Thank you, Uncle George Hu, Assistant to the Governor of New York State for Asian Affairs. Your care and concern have been keeping me company. You have helped me to realize that my dream will come true so long as I have a dream and constantly strive for it. Thank you, Brother Yao Ming. We have got to know you as a wise brother rather than a famous basketball player. I am convinced that the China 150 will be sure to do our bit for the Yao Foundation. Thank you, Chinese Americans. We have learned from you the power of unity and that we Chinese maintain flesh and blood ties with our motherland wherever we are.

With Mother Kathy at the Consulate-General of the P. R. C. in New York in May, 2009

You are the ones with a different skin color who have made us fully understand what " One World, One Dream" really means. Thank you, Mother Kathy, the Director of Communication of SUNY - Farmingdale State College. Your maternal love has flattened the boundaries and warmed our heart. From time to time, we think of your words: "I don't know what I'm gonna do when these kids leave. " Your eyes were red when you said this. Thank you, Dr. Keen, President of SUNY - Farmingdale State College. You have treated us like stars, inviting us to your house and playing volleyball and games like "concentration" with us. Thank you, Lorraine, Dean of the Business School. Your charm, optimism and enthusiasm have made me realize that life is always full of sunshine. Thank you, Professor Marrone. You are always proud to introduce me like this: "This is my second daughter." Thank you, dear professors and teachers. Your caring and watering make me more eager to blossom.

We are the sprouting buds, being cared for and growing vigorously...

As members of the China 150, we are justified to be proud of ourselves because we have successfully completed our mission—serving as a link between Sino-American cultural exchanges. We did it! This is best exemplified by the two-hour Chinese Culture Show which has been organized and staged by the Farmingdale 19. I know we have made it when hundreds of people watching the show were learning Chinese with us, when the flash lamps kept flashing during the show, when the president presented me with flowers (as I was the chief organizer and director), when we received high praises from the audience, when American friends stood in a long line for being given a Chinese name, when everyone gave high praises while tasting Chinese food and when everyone was eager to know more about Chinese culture. I am

At the home of Dr. Keen, president of SUNY – Farmingdale State College, on Aug. 31, 2008

convinced that so long as we work hard together, we are bound to succeed sooner or later.

In the Public Speaking class, I successfully talked my classmates into learning Chinese. When the professor remarked like this, "You are a wonderful ambassador for your country," I began to fully understand the saying "Where there is will, there is a way." When we were busy

introducing China at the Asian-American Culture Festival of Long Island, when we were invited to introduce more Chinese culture to American kids at school, I knew we could influence more people with our efforts. When we were expressing our gratitude on the performance stages at Columbia University and Princeton University, I realized that we had been overwhelmed with love in this year. Consequently, as we volunteer to participate in public benefit activities, I am completely aware that we can pass on the love we have received to more people...

If buds are growing larger, can blossoms be far away?

One step forward, two hearts closer. The connection built by love lasts forever...

Yin Jing, from Deyang City, Sichuan Province.

I study Insurance at Southwestern University of Finance and Economics. During my nine months in the US, I went to SUNY - Farmingdale State College, majoring in Business Management.

Striving for My Dream with a Grateful Heart

By Tan Miao

Southwestern University of Finance and Economics

How time flies! Almost a year has passed since the Wenchuan Earthquake and the arrival of us in the USA from the severely afflicted areas in Sichuan Province. Being concerned about my hometown every single day, I always felt relieved to learn about the ongoing reconstruction from my father. In the meantime, I kept wondering what contributions I could make to the reconstruction.

Far away in the United States we have been cherishing these thoughts in our own ways. We are lucky, for we are the hope of our dear folks back in Sichuan Province and we witness Sino-American friendship. Ever since we came to the United States, we have been experiencing a life different from that of other international students. Like several others, I was appointed to study at SUNY − Farmingdale State College, which is a technical college located in a special area, Long Island, in New York City. We have participated in a variety of public benefit activities on behalf of the China 150, through which we have learned a lot and benefited enormously. In New York City, we witness the prosperity of this great American financial city, while in Washington D. C. we are impressed by the solemn atmosphere of the capital and the culture-saturated layout of buildings.

It has been an eventful year for us as well as for the Americans: the global financial crisis, the election of Obama as the nation's first African American president and Premier Wen Jiabao's visit of the United Nations. We are constantly made aware of the fact that our Motherland is prosperous and influential. Americans are showing great interest in China.

They respect us and think highly of the wisdom of us Chinese. Many American friends have made it known that the international situation largely depends on the relationship between China and the United States.

In Farmingdale, we have an "American Mother" whose name is Kathy. She has a deep love for us, the nineteen Chinese students from the earthquake-stricken area. This is what she said about us: "They are the most polite and smart students I have ever seen." She would quietly listen to what had happened during the Wenchuan Earthquake, tears in her eyes. Moreover, she would ask us about the details of our special interview by the Hunan Satellite TV Station. What's more, she would invite us to her house at the festivals and even try to cook her dishes like Sichuan food. In a word, she respected us and took great efforts to make us feel at ease. She was constantly thinking what she could do for us and for Sichuan. As the anniversary of the Wenchuan Earthquake was drawing near, Kathy proposed to the school authority that we, the Farmingdale 19, plant a special tree in the garden on the campus of SUNY – Farmingdale State College in memory of our dear family members and friends who died in the terrible disaster and the devastation of the land where we spent our happy childhood and to commemorate our stay in Farmingdale because of the earthquake.

There is one thing that we take great pride in. To show our gratitude to the beloved American friends, to the Chinese Americans and to the staff members of the Consulate-General of the People's Republic of China in New York, we, the Farmingdale 19, staged a two-hour Chinese Culture Show on our own. This show demonstrated Chinese calligraphy, food,

My performance at the Chinese Culture Show

dress, adornment, instrumental music, dance and social etiquette. We organized and prepared everything for the show from lighting, music, performance, choreography, PPT, video, and interactive activities to curtains, propaganda, invitations, etc. All the professors and students present at the show were deeply impressed and amazed. They marveling at the joint efforts of the Farmingdale 19; the comprehensive and profound Chinese culture; the fast development of science and technology and the modernization of China. When the Chinese Culture Show ended with a Chorus "Welcome to China," all the audience stood up and clapped, with a deafening thunderous applause. At that very moment, we were burning with righteous ardor and were moved to tears. At that very moment, a national pride emerged from the deepest of my heart, touching every part of me. An American Chinese TV station made a special report of our show and the Dean of the Business School of SUNY – Farmingdale State College remarked like this: "This is the most fabulous show I have ever watched on campus for ten years."

On the first day of the Chinese Lunar New Year Day, a few of the China 150 were lucky to meet and talk with Yao Ming. He is not only a basketball star but also a banner, because to many Americans Yao is the image representative of us Chinese as he embodies the typical Chinese virtues of wisdom, persistence and modesty. This meeting fully shows Yao Ming's concern for the earthquake-stricken area in Sichuan Province. After learning that the Yao Foundation has planned to build five Hope Primary Schools in the earthquake-hit area in Sichuan Province, I and other nineteen representatives of the China 150 expressed our wish to set up a special committee of volunteers for the Hope Primary Schools. During the meeting I made a detailed description of the badly damaged primary schools in my hometown, Shifang, hoping that Yao Ming would make use of his influence to call on more people to help the kids who had to quit their study due to the earthquake in my hometown.

The time is drawing near when I go back to China. My heart has already gone back to my motherland. After my return, I will be completely new and different, sharing my trip to America with my family,

fellow students and friends, going on to fulfill my dreams...

We are sure that the China 150 are 150 new seeds, sowed in August last year and fully grown in the past nine months. We will pass on hope in the future reconstruction!

Dream big, devote more; seize opportunities, improve much; position myself, and enjoy life.

Tan Miao, from Shifang City, Sichuan Province.

I study at Southwestern University of Finance and Economics. During my nine months in the US, I studied at SUNY – Farmingdale State College.

My Life as an International Student in the United States
—A Year of Harvest

By Zhang Rui

University of Electronic Science and Technology of China

Whether I like it or not, my story began with the May 12 earthquake. I thought that I had gone through various kinds of situations during the past twenty years of my growing up; in particular, returning to high school after I failed the college entrance examination made me truly understand the joys and sorrows of life. I thought I had experienced enough to help me calmly face whatever happened and overcome all sorts of difficulties. However, the moment the earthquake befell us, I realized how trivial and useless I was. I know many people shared this feeling. This is probably why the media regard this earthquake as a test and education of the post-80s generation in China.

I have to say I am fortunate because all my family members have survived the catastrophe, but I have learned one thing: to cherish friendship, family relationship and my future love.

I have been wondering what has happened to me. If I had not reentered high school after failing the college entrance examination, I would not have got this chance to study in the United States because juniors are not entitled to this program. Had not the teachers and the student advisor in my school recommended me, it would not have been possible for me to know about this program at the earliest possible time and time time thereby to get an interview. Is this fate? I do not know.

This one year in the United State is a dictionary to me which includes too many things to chew over and take in. Some things take quite some time to ponder, while others are as digestible as liquid diets. Talking about the past year, I will not hesitate to say: I have got to know different cultures; I have realized how colorful the world is; I have improved my English and enhanced the basic skills of listening, speaking, reading and writing; I have bettered my social skills; I have been impressed by the concern of American friends, Chinese Americans and our motherland; and so on. To be sure, all theses are true, but what matters to me most is a change of the philosophy of life.

One should be grateful, which is what I say time and time again on many occasions. Over the past twenty years, I have never felt so strongly how subtle and intriguing human beings are. Some covet small advantages by whatever means possible, while somebody else sold the house which he/she had bought by tightening the belt for most of his/her life just to help those kids in mountainous areas, who had dropped out of school due to poverty. Have you ever thought about the reason behind this? I often thought about this while in America. The answer is not hard to find. Everyone should decide his own destiny. While man is born with equal rights, rights to seek profits and pleasure, he is not obliged to help others unselfishly. Consequently, there is no right and wrong with regard to his/her behavior. What matters is his/her philosophy of life: to enjoy life and be egoistic or to help others and be altruistic. He/She is really free to choose. Therefore when someone lends you a hand, do remember this: it is not his/her responsibility; you should be grateful rather than take it for granted.

With Kathy on May 12, 2009 in memory of the earthquake

Kathy is agreeable and easy to get along with. Because of her sweet smile, consideration and care, we, the Farmingdale 19, call her "American Mom. " Indeed, while we were in the States, she did lots of things for us and took care of us like a mom. It is hard to imagine that she even remembered to hold a birthday party for each of us, which was really special when we were far away from home in a strange land. She witnessed our growing up day by day.

With Victoria after the last talk in May

We intended to get a part-time job at the Career Development Center of our college but were disappointed that there was no vacancy. However, a week later we got an email from the center asking us whether we would like to do voluntary work. We readily consented because we could do something for others. This voluntary job enabled us to make a new friend. We worked under Victoria Ripley who was a postgraduate at Columbia University and working at SUNY − Maritime College. Being a career development counselor was her practical training. Our main task was to help her publicize a website, distributing leaflets at such places as the library twice a week. At first we were like strangers for we seldom had the chance to talk with each other. Later on, the publicity campaign was suspended. Since we had nothing to do, she proposed that we have a free talk twice a week. One of us would choose a different topic each time, the purpose of which was to get to know our different cultures, thus enabling us to adapt to the American way of life as soon as possible. Our talk covered almost everything we could think of, from the names of vegetables, consumption tax to educational ideals. What impressed us most was her remark during our talk about the behavior of different nations: "Do not interfere with others so long as you are not harmed by their behavior. Everybody is free to do what he likes." This is perhaps one of the most useful things I have learnt in America because it makes me become more tolerant of others.

There is one more thing that has impressed me most: how to find what you are interested in and go all out for it. I have a host family.

My host is an American and my
hostess is from Taiwan whose name
is Suiv Lee. As I was often invited
to my host family, we chatted a
lot. Suiv is talkative and enjoys
sharing her experiences and
opinions. I came to learn about her
family, her work experiences and
her children she takes so much pride
in. Her work experiences fascinate

With Suiv Lee at the graduation in May

me a lot: she came to the United States when she was only a small child.
After innumerable hardships she graduated from university and began to
wander around the United States. She did various jobs and once even
worked at a casino in Las Vegas. Later she came to New York and set up
a computer company which became increasingly prosperous. Like in her
previous jobs, she soon became tired of it though the company was quite
profitable. It was not the very job that she had longed to have. Then one
day she decided to be a teacher and became helplessly in love with it.
Now she is very much fascinated with the job and teaches at two
universities. In January this year, she began to pursue her doctorial studies
at the Teachers College of Columbia University although she had to pay
quite a lot of tuition fees. What strikes me most is how to find out what
one is interested in and accomplish self-realization.

Like many Chinese here, we went to the church to see what it was
like. When the priest learned about us from the newspaper, he visited us,
provided overcoats for us, and went mountain climbing with us. We went
to the homes of many church members. I was especially impressed by Lu
Yitai, a team leader. He came from Taiwan and works as a professor in
the School of Science and Technology, New York University. He has to
walk with sticks because one of his legs is disabled. However, he is the
most cheerful among the members. Though disabled, he is unexpectedly
proficient in skiing. He even has a professional skiing coaching license and
often drives to the skiing resorts. He derived much pleasure from it and

told us his stories of skiing time and time again. In addition, he is keen on such activities as catching crabs and going fishing in the sea. In a word, he is hardly affected by his physical defect. On the contrary, he knows better than many healthy people how to enjoy life and how to cope with difficulties in an optimistic way.

There is one topic that must be touched on. We never forget we are Chinese. In the eyes of the Americans, Chinese students are synonymous to "top students" and "hard workers." In a foreign country, we are not only individual students, but also the image of China. Naturally our behavior will affect the opinion of others about China. Therefore it goes without saying it is our duty to work hard, make great progress and bring credit to all overseas Chinese students. Within less than one year, all the professors at SUNY – Farmingdale State College realized that we Chinese students are dependable, diligent; and we have a good command of the basic skills and excel in mathematics. Everyone spoke highly of Chinese students, which undoubtedly made us confident and aware of the advantages of tertiary education in China. The same is true of Chinese in American political circles. I have a tutor here, George Hu, who is from Shanghai and now serves as Assistant to the Governor of New York State. He came to study in the United States when he was a teenager. He caught the attention of the governor when his proposal for taxation put forward while still in university was adopted by the state government, thereby beginning his political life. As an assistant, he is in charge of Asian affairs. Because he always remembers he is a Chinese, he shuttles back and forth between the state government and Chinatown. He works for the interests of the local Chinese, helping them with employment and bringing them tangible benefits. This may seem

Celebrating the Mid-Autumn Festival with George Hu, Assistant to the Governor of New York State in Farmingdale State College

easy, but it is by no means easy to do so for decades. In a word, we should never forget we are Chinese.

Looking back on this year in the United States, I find I have benefited a great deal and there are lots of things which are hard to forget, which will perhaps change my life.

Opportunities are for those who are well-prepared.

Zhang Rui, from Mianyang City, Sichuan Province.

I study at University of Electronic Science and Technology of China. During my nine months in the US, I studied at SUNY – Farmingdale State College.

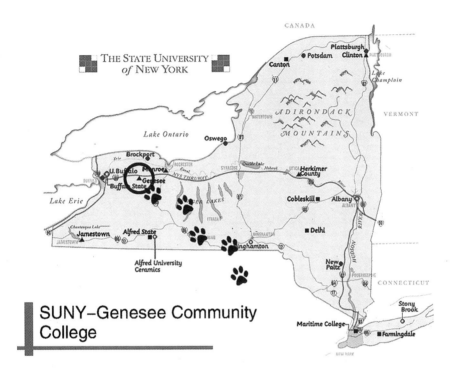

SUNY–Genesee Community
College

"A Touchdown" in the United States

By Sun Chen
University of Electronic Science and Technology of China

I was offered an interview for the CSC-SUNY 150 Program at a time when I remembered well the violent and devastating shake of the Wenchuan Earthquake which took place on May 12, 2008, when I still seemed to hear the sad desperate cries and moans, and when pictures of collapsed houses still remained fresh in my mind. I went all out for this opportunity of a lifetime. After passing the interview given by the University of Electronic Science and Technology of China and China Scholarship Council, I won the scholarship of the State University of New York and was going to be an international student. This soothed my grief-stricken heart and cheered me up. I, together with 149 other fellow students, set out on my journey to the United States bearing in mind the hope and expectations of my dear folks and motherland.

Here I am!

I was extremely excited when I arrived because this was the first time for me to come to America. As soon as we got off the plane, we saw friendly smiles of the local people waiting for us and no longer felt worried or uneasy. We arrived at SUNY − Maritime College, received a warm welcome and enjoyed a rich delicious meal. Though it was raining hard with lightening and thunder, we felt cozy and warm. We got round New York City by bus the following day. There were too many tourist attractions for the eye to take in. Luckily, we had an "uncle" with us who explained everything to us in Chinese, and this really made it most rewarding to us new comers. Later on we visited the Chinatown. The warm reception from compatriots made us feel nice and comfortable. Finally we arrived at the Consulate-General of the People's Republic of China in New York and met the teachers from various colleges of the State University of New York. We set off for the different colleges and began our new life as overseas students the day after.

With English teacher Charley Boyd at Chocolate Factory in Batavia

The Beautiful Countryside

The SUNY – Genesee Community College where I studied is situated at Batavia, Genesee County, New York. New York is mainly agricultural in nature and this makes New York City unique among the large cities. When the eight of us Chinese students arrived at the place where we were going to live for nine months, what came into our view was not the heavy traffic nor tall buildings as expected but an endless stretch of farm land and cows wandering about in the fields. This is just like the country music which I enjoy most, and this is my favorite way of life. Far away from the hubbub of New York City, we are rewarded with blue sky, fresh air and smiling faces everywhere.

Though in the countryside, the college is full of facilities of every sort. One phenomenon that is very common in America is that the best building in a town is the school building. There is only one teaching building at SUNY – Genesee Community College. It houses a gymnasium and even a swimming pool. It is really an all-in-one building.

Hello! How Are You?

As we got used to the life here and improved our listening and speaking, we had more contact with others. The loose and favorable policy of Genesee Community College attracts students from all over the world. In our contacts with other overseas students of various personalities from different countries, we got to know their cultures and customs. What's more, we learned all sorts of new ideas and thoughts from them.

In America, people can talk freely whatever country you are from. A simple hello can start a conversation between strangers as if they were friends. During my stay here, I often went to parties with other fellow students. We also played sports and games together. I realized there were no such things as color and language barriers. Friendship just needs honesty and tolerance.

Looking out into the Future

Undoubtedly there is a big gap between America, the superpower in the world, and China, a fast developing country.

While I was here in the United States, I witnessed the gap, but felt confident and hopeful. So long as we study hard, work diligently, and strive continuously to make new progress, we are bound to shorten the gap and catch up.

Farewell

How time flies! As the saying goes, "The longest day has its end. " The time finally came when we had to say goodbye.

We had to leave though we were quite reluctant, because our friends and family members right across the ocean had been looking forward to our return.

This long journey is like a touchdown in American football. I have already left my footprints here in America. I will go back to my motherland and embrace the dawn of victory.

More than one year has passed before I once again set foot on the soil of my hometown. I am no longer gloomy and depressed. As I see the reconstruction going on everywhere, I know this is not an end, but rather a new beginning.

Hopes accompany me always!

Sun Chen, from Aba Tibetan and Qiang Autonomous Prefecture, Sichuan Province.

I study Communicating Engineering at University of Electronic Science and Technology of China. In America, I studied Engineering Science at SUNY - Genesee Community College.

Journey to America

By Lü Hongjiang
University of Electronic Science and Technology of China

Building up Confidence

We went on an orientation tour on our own the first day we arrived at the SUNY – Genesee Community College. As we came to the Student Union, I was excited to find that there were two table tennis tables. Just at that moment, the president walked toward us, with a smile on his face. He asked us if we'd like to play a few games with him and we readily agreed.

Once the game began, the president beat two of our best players. I had heard that he was called "table tennis president" and he turned out to be quite skillful and defeated his opponents without much effort. It was quite possible that he had not played to the best of his ability. He was a real challenge and I took my bat from my school bag, ready to go all out. Unexpectedly, as he was only able to defend himself but unable to hit back, I beat the president.

Playing basketball on campus

After defeating the president, I began to feel a little confident, thinking I could beat others in one field or another. As I played more and more with other students here, I found the president was truly the most skilled among those I had played with. Later on, we realized that we were remarkably outstanding in many

195

sports. My fellow Chinese students were top players of billiards and badminton. We were even able to rival other students in basketball.

What made me really confident was the excellent results in our studies. We, the six Chinese boy students, at SUNY − Genesee Community College chose the same courses. At first, lectures in English were quite difficult for me but I managed to understand the knowledge and skills taught by the teacher. Only then did I fully realize that mathematics is a kind of language. Whether in assignments or in examinations, the lowest marks we got were more than ninety points.

In autumn, 2008, our teacher asked us to take part in a mathematics competition. All the students in the junior colleges in the state, who chose mathematics, were eligible for the competition. We participated in the competition only for extra credits. Later, our teacher was very excited to tell me that I ranked the second of all the students in the state, which came as a severe shock to me. Though I was average in mathematics back in China, I was unexpectedly strong here in America. In spring, 2009, we took part in this competition again. This time we prepared ourselves for the competition and practiced answering all the questions from previous competitions during the past few years. When the results came out, we got e-mails from many teachers congratulating us. Because of our excellent performance, our college ranked first. I myself got the full marks and another fellow student ranked third in the state.

At that moment, I really built up my confidence.

Learning to Cook Chinese Food in America

It sounds incredible that I learned to cook Chinese food in America. There is a small restaurant on campus but it is somewhat expensive. The scholarship was given to us in a rather interesting way. We altogether had a weekly budget of $500. Every week our adviser Amy would take us to Wal-Mart and bought what we would need for a week. At first I was at a loss what to buy and how much I ought to buy. During the first few months, we tried all types of food in the supermarket. As we no longer wanted to eat bread, hamburgers and hot dogs, someone suggested we cook food ourselves.

The four boys in our bedroom had never cooked meals, except helping with cooking at most. As for me, I could only cook instant noodles. What should we do? We did something quite funny. You know what? We watched and tried to learn cooking from a cartoon *Cooking Master*! Cooking was not so difficult after all and we began to try cooking. We immediately realized that the fast cutting up of vegetables and slicing of meat in the cartoon was dramatized. We started to cut up vegetables with a small knife and it was terribly slow. What's more, there were no spices except salt and soy source. After an endless hour, our first dish, stir-fried pork with cucumber slices, was ready. It was really delicious although now we know it was far from tasty.

After a couple of weeks' trial and error, we were able to cook such homely dishes like Stir-Fried Shredded Pork with Green Pepper, Chopped Pork with Vermicelli, Stir-Fried Shrimps with Cauliflower, Stir-Fried Pork with Cucumber Slices. My main job was to slice pork with scissors. It is both inconvenient and a bit dangerous to use a kitchen knife. In contrast, it is both easier and more quickly for me to cut meat into the desirable size with scissors. Using scissors may appear to be funny but it is indeed efficient.

By and by, cooking brought us a lot of pleasure.

Studying in the United States

The American interest-oriented education differs greatly from either test-oriented education or quality-oriented education. The Americans believe that every one is born with different abilities, so the function of primary schools and junior middle schools is to help students discover their inborn talents and encourage them to pursue their own interest. Let's look at one example. If a boy says he wants to be a baker when he grows up, in China he will get a tongue-lashing from his teachers and parents, reminding him that other kids want to be scientists or calligraphers and

blaming him for a lack of great ambition, while in America teachers and parents will be happy to know what he wants to be in the future. They will find relevant books, buy various baking equipments and even take him to a bakery.

This education ideal is shown in the freedom to choose majors and courses in American universities. Once a student decides on a major, he goes to a student advisor who recommends courses for him. Besides it is quite easy for him to change his major. What he needs to do is to simply choose some other courses in the next term.

The advantage of interest-oriented education is that students can learn what they are interested in and this motivates them to learn actively. As a result, it is easy to cultivate a wide range of talents.

The make-up of a student's academic results is different from that in China. Each term home assignments or quizzes account for a large proportion while the final exam makes up only 20% to 30%.

The focus on the regular grade during the term rather than the final exam results reflects the goal of education—enabling students to really learn knowledge. Learning is an accumulative step-by-step process. Once a problem appears, · you should solve it in time. Otherwise, there will be increasingly more problems waiting to be solved.

In America, when the marked test papers are handed out to the students in class, what's worth mentioning is that the teacher always lets the side with the mark face downward so that other students can not see it. Even if you do poorly in the exam, the teacher will not tell the class. Everyone only knows his own score.

They regard the exam results as a kind of privacy. In China there will be a ranking whether it is a quiz or exam. Those at the top are triumphantly proud while those at the bottom are embarrassingly discouraged. The initial intent is that when we see men of worth, we should think of equaling them. Thus, students have a role model. However, it turns out to be the opposite. Because learning is an accumulative process and it is hard to make a breakthrough in a short period of time. It is almost impossible for those at the bottom to catch up.

As for those at the bottom, this kind of ranking is disheartening to them and makes them feel no matter how hard they work they can hardly do better. They gradually give up study and spend their time and energy on such things like games and sports which will make them feel confident. Ranking does no good to those at the top, either. First, their parents are likely to show them off to other parents who in turn use them as positive examples to educate their children. The result is that younger students will be jealous of those at the top rather than think of how to catch up with them. Consequently, top students play with other top students while slow students enjoy playing with other slow students. Secondly, it is likely for top students to have a misunderstanding that good performance deserves praise and they are superior to others. They may easily become arrogant and conceited, which makes it difficult for them to get on well with others and make friends.

Final exams are held at a test center. The teacher sets a period of time, say, one week, during which you may take the exam on any day so that you will be in your best state. After telling the staff there the name of the course you have chosen and the name of the teacher, you go into a classroom and begin your exam. In case you can't make the set time, you may talk it over with your teacher and ask if it is possible to take the exam at an earlier date. Occasionally the teacher may even allow you to take the test paper home and hand it in the next day. Honesty and trust are thus fully demonstrated. Think it over and you know that plagiarism does you no good except cheating yourself. Honesty is a basic personal qualities. It is even so in your studies. If one is found of plagiarism or cheating on the exam, he will get no score for this course. It takes years to gain credibility. Once it is lost, it is difficult to win it back. A man without honesty and credibility will get nowhere in the society. It may not seem so serious to get a zero mark in an examination but when you begin to find a job and if you have a record of plagiarism or cheating on the exam, it is almost likely that nobody will hire you.

Such an educational system has made me understand the following: First, study is your own business rather than a business of the school, parents or teachers; second, you must study hard and seriously as there is no point in cheating. Only by learning actively and in earnest can you make real progress and derive pleasure from it.

Lü Hongjiang, from Mianyang City, Sichuan Province.

I am a student in UESTC (University of Electronic Science and Technology of China), majoring in Communication Engineering. After the nine months in SUNY – Genesee Community College, I feel that I have grown up. I have the confidence to face the challenges in my life and studies.

Faramita Flower

By Wang Dan
Sichuan Normal University

Faramita, the flower of life, blooms on the other side of the ocean....

August 15, 2008, was an unusual and unforgettable day in my life.

I, an ordinary student from Sichuan Normal University, came to the States all the way across the North Pole, across the Pacific Ocean, by a international airliner with 149 fellow students.

We were exhausted after such a cross-the-ocean flight, but we were excited and kept looking forward to our life abroad.

My First Days in New York

We stayed on the campus of Maritime College of SUNY the very first day we arrived in New York. Facing the sea the campus is so beautiful, with a cross-sea bridge ahead. It was my first experience like this and it was just marvelous. On the campus, there are also forts left by the American Force in the World War II, as well as a navy base.

For the first time, I saw the sea; for the first time, I saw the navy warship; and for the first time, I smelt the air of a foreign land.

We went to the Chinatown in Manhattan the next day. The Chinese people in the States treated us with great hospitality in the Golden Bridge Restaurant and gave each of us $50 as pocket money in a red envelope. It was so exciting to receive pocket money in dollars. We felt at home with so many Chinese accompanying us.

We visited the Consulate-General of the P. R. C. in New York. The

Consul General and his wife treated us warmly, and the presidents from different campuses of SUNY and representatives of teachers met us for the first time there. It was a parting day as well as a happy start, a start for adventure!

After an eight-hour bus ride, the eight of us reached our final destination—Genesee Community College. Many student representatives came to meet us, gave us loads of gifts and helped carrying our luggage to the dorm. We found the basic necessities, ranging from quilt to stationeries such as pens, scissors, notebooks and glue, were prepared for us and we felt extremely warm.

We met our tutor, a cute, slim and beautiful American teacher, at the Student Union. She and her boss Margaret prepared the most popular American food for us, such as yogurt, oatmeal, chips, dessert, hot dogs, toast and so on, and asked us to pick out the ones we liked so that we knew what to buy in Wal-Mart.

Several days later, a kind leader named Tarnya came to see us and taught us to cook American dishes. All of us liked this kind lady who always has a warm smile on her face and who has great passion. What a nice teacher!

The sky here is so close to the land, so blue and so beautiful.

We had grass land around our campus, and a big farm opposite our dorm, thereafter we often felt the smell of cows—the smell of farm! I love the environment here on the farm, which is so nice, so fresh and so quiet.

Sweet Blooming

Not long after the opening ceremony, the university president invited us to take part in the yearly Teachers Meeting, in which the excellent teacher in the year would be elected and it was my first time to attend an American party.

We went to many barbecues organized by the school as well. They were fun and with much delicious food, such as grilled meat, hot dogs and ice cream.

Gradually we mingled in the routine studies and the local life in the States.

I got along well with my roommate, who was nice and often gave me help. I made some friends at school. Two of them were Japanese girls. They studied very hard and treated others very sincerely.

I studied hard and read carefully. With so many new words in the reading, I often spent several hours on one reading assignment, but I benefited a lot and felt that my knowledge was enriched.

We would cook some Sichuan dishes to have the feeling of home when we missed home.

Our English teacher, Mr. Boyd, was just like our uncle who taught us to carve pumpkins on Halloween and to paint eggs on Easter Day. He often showed us around. We went to Buffalo, Rochester, Niagara Falls, Darien Lake, Batavia Chocolate Factory and many other interesting places. We got so much selfless help from him and his wife, which we appreciated so much.

Our tutor, Amy, always took us to Wal-Mart the same time every week for shopping. It was a great favor for us, who had no means of transportation.

In winter, we went to Washington D. C. for a special training program and more than sixty members of China 150 took part in the program. We visited the Capitol Hill, Washington Monument, and the White House and discussed issues with senior officials. We learned a lot and displayed our personalities and wisdom.

Time flew. Soon came the second semester.

Our school paid more attention to the spreading of Chinese culture. A Chinese Year activity was held on campus in February, 2009. Americans were invited to try the Chinese dishes, listen to Chinese songs, and enjoy the Dragon Play. A Chinese Picture Show was held in the same month. It was an exhibition of collections and photos from China offered by Josephine, who had taught in China before. In March, Chinese Teahouse was held by the school and many American people enjoyed the

tea culture of China. We gave each of them a unique Chinese name. We are proud we are Chinese.

At that moment, we realized we were not there for studies only. We were also there to spread Chinese culture.

The eight of us voluntarily worked as "envoys" to teach our American friends Chinese. We worked on two shifts, one group taught during the day while the other taught in the evening. We planned the classes in advance and printed handouts for our "students." We felt rewarded when we saw them study hard and heard them read seriously.

They were such lovely "students." In the last class they brought some homemade food, such as salad, dessert, jam and mashed potatoes, to show their appreciation to us for teaching them Chinese. Though the food was not expensive and the classroom was not magnificent, we felt their genuine sincerity. It was a Final Party I'll never forget.

Karin, an administrative staff member of the university who studied Chinese with us, wrote us a formal appreciation letter with her and the university vice president's signatures on it. I felt extremely flattered.

Consul General Peng Keyu came to Buffalo to visit us and had a talk with us, in which we shared hardships and gains.

My flower of life bloomed brilliantly there....

Reluctant Parting

May 21, 2009 was the day for us to leave the Genesee Community College.

Our teachers, Amy, Karin, Josephine, Margaret and many others came to say goodbye. There were no tears but laughter. What I said most that day was, "I'm gonna miss you." That is true. I am going to miss each of you there.

Again, we took the international airliner. What made it different from last time was that, this time it took us away from New York, away from the States.

Goodbye, New York. I am going to start a new lap of journey in my life. I am going to miss you. I have seen so much, experienced so much and learned so much. Each of the people I encountered will be kept in my memory. I learned to be independent, I learned to be tolerant and I learned to memorize and appreciate the kindness from others. I appreciate everyone who appeared in my life, and I appreciate everyone who has helped me and loved me. I will cherish the sweet memory in the States. I will go on with my striving.

Thank you, China! Thank you, New York!

It was you who made my flower of life bloom on the other side of the ocean.

Thanks to all the people who have given me love and help!

Wang Dan, from Dujiangyan City, Sichuan Province.

In China, I study at Geography and Resource Sciences College of Sichuan Normal University. From September 2008 to May 2009, I studied at Resources Environment and the Management of Urban and Rural Planning of SUNY – Genesee Community College.

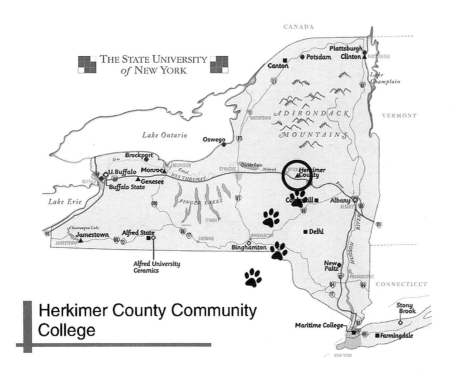

THE STATE UNIVERSITY
of NEW YORK

Herkimer County Community College

Enjoying Growing Pain

By Chen Wenbi
China West Normal University

CSC-SUNY 150 Program is a miracle, created with love by thousands of people after May 12 Wenchuan Earthquake. It has become the most precious memory of the children growing up on this land.

—for the memory of our days in America

On August 17, 2008, in two cottages on Prospect Street in a small town called Herkimer, eleven students from earthquake-stricken area of China embarked on their one-year life in America. This is how it all begins. Amid the language barrier, we all felt lonely and homesick in a strange environment. But at least we could learn to cook together, starting from Scrambled Eggs with Tomato to Sweet and Sour Spareribs. We walked in bitterly cold winter, carrying loads of stuff we bought from the supermarket. We slipped on the stiff ice, helplessly staring at our stained clothes as well as crashed eggs and milk on the icy ground. We went to parties together... We went through those lonely times together. It was in this course of event that I gained precious friendship for we are the friends who are always together, from the very beginning of a day to the very end. We suffered a lot together. We are the friends of life, the life of growing up.

It was after I arrived in America when I realized that every single word and deed of mine does not only reflect my own personality, but also represent my country and people. Whatever I did, I tried to be better. Every time I heard compliments like "Chinese students are excellent," I felt very proud and therefore motivated to be better in my coursework.

My one-year study here was both fulfilling and fun. Public speaking availed me the opportunity to face my fears. At first I always stammered in front of a large group of Americans. As time passed by, my public speaking skills were gradually perfected and my teacher even photocopied my presentation drafts as her reference for future teaching. Apart from speaking skills, also honed was my courage and confidence. The seemingly simple Story Telling was a course that trained our way of expression and tested understanding of our own culture. Instead of reciting a story, we presented the live stories to everybody in our unique way. Story selection was the most painful process, because I always wanted to choose from many versions the one that was most representative of the brilliant Chinese culture. Then I translated them into English. Understanding of American Culture was one of my favorite courses. The teachers took us to many places to experience American culture.

International dinner with other international students

I also took part in an honor program where the students could choose their preferred tutors as well as research topics of their own interested subjects. I chose Health Care. I collected lots of data from the Internet, and interviewed local doctors, nurses, people in charge, and government officials, before writing a term paper on the difference between Chinese and American Health Care Systems. I have gained a lot from such fulfilling and fun study life.

Besides study, my extracurricular activities were also colorful. We took part in students' societies and organized events with classmates from different countries. Once we, together with several American students, successfully mixed up a healthy drink by blending Chinese tea with American beverage. Sometimes our teachers invited us to their homes to have barbecue. We cooked with other international students. A feast of dishes featuring different countries was like a culture communication on food.

Traveling was also an important part of our life here. During one special trip (we considered it a New Year gift to ourselves), my friend and I went backpacking around New York City with only a camera, a map and a small amount of cash on us. I still remember it was past

Making Jack-o'-Lanterns at teacher's house at Halloween

4 a. m. when we arrived at the city. With some help, we tumbled on subway at a little past 5 a. m. That was the first time I toured through a strange city without any tour guide, but only a map. I became aware that in order to get to know the culture and life of a city, the best way is to read neither pompous guide books nor travelogues by well-known writers, but to be in the city savoring its beauty.

Doing voluntary work was also a major component of our lives in America. We taught Chinese in primary schools, helped to wash dishes in churches, told stories to the elderly in rest homes... We just wanted to pass on our love and care.

This year was not merely a year of gaining insight into American culture; it also offered me an opportunity to ponder over my own brilliant culture before imparting it to someone else. We often encountered some touchy problems like Taiwan issue and Tibet issue. I still remember once when I was asked, "Is Tibet a part of China?" "Of course, " I replied

Teaching Chinese at a primary school as a volunteer

angrily. I couldn't understand why they could have asked such an ignorant question. Isn't it common sense? Haven't they learned geography? It was until later that I found out that most Americans do not know China well. Ever since then we tried our best to explain that China is an inseparable territory. I discovered that, after my one-year stay in America, I became more attached to my motherland than ever before. Anything can be appreciated more after you truly understand it. It was during this process of learning and explaining that I gradually realized my deep affection, a most simple, spontaneous affection to my own nation. One of my classmates said it was like in our childhood, when we often complained about our mothers' cooking. But when the neighboring children discredited a single bit of our mothers' cooking, we couldn't help defending our moms, sometimes even fought with the kid. Although our country still has many problems, we sometimes still complain about its poor social system and corruption practice, we would never tolerate it being criticized. We love our country. We know every country has its own problems. It has not been easy for our country to achieve such rapid development after it encountered so many historical problems. She has been successful. This one-year experience in America is a process of not only getting to know a foreign culture, but also of recognizing and spreading our culture. I am very grateful that I had this opportunity to perceive my motherland from a different perspective, thus realizing how deeply I am bound up with her.

My one-year American life is unforgettable, with everything worth recalling. All my memories of feeling lost, feeling lonely, shedding tears, bursting out laughter, experiencing changes and harvesting friendship became the most memorable and happiest part of my life. I was once asked, "What is your biggest harvest in this year?" While most people would say English fluency, I, on the other hand, believe it is maturity. I learned how to take good care of myself; how to get along with others, with people from diverse culture backgrounds. I learned to express gratitude, and to study independently. I learned to be the person I want to be with the courage to pursue my dream. I learned to rely on myself and face all obstacles on my own, instead of waiting for help. I learned the importance of my country to myself. Perhaps one year's exposure to English-speaking environment is not long enough for me to speak English fluently, or really understand American culture, or become a wholly independent brave person. However, I gained knowledge, friendship as well as courage. I am contented, as every member of China 150. I would like to express my heartfelt thanks to this program, to those who worked hard for it, and to those who extended us their warmest hands along our journey. I also feel grateful for having this opportunity to have our stories in America published. It provides us a platform to tell our stories to everybody, as well as a chance to recollect and reflect our pieces of lives in America. Suddenly I found myself growing up—painfully yet happily.

We are the friends who are always together, from the very beginning of a day to the very end. We suffered a lot together. We are the friends of life.

Chen Wenbi, from Wenchuan County, Sichuan Province.

I study English Education at China West Normal University. From 2008 to 2009, I studied English Language and Literature at Herkimer County Community College.

My American Dream

By Yuan Yue
Chengdu University of Technology

I have dreamed of going abroad ever since I was a little girl, for I love those adorable dolls, yearn for candy houses in *Andersen's Fairy Tales*, and dream of having fun in Disneyland. I have always wanted to explore the birthplace of those dreamy fairy tales. As I grew up, I began to learn English, listen to English songs, watch English movies, and rehearse English dramas. I enjoyed all these enriching activities, while at the same time, my long-cherished going-abroad dream faded faintly, for I can experience all I have wanted in my own country. I can strike up a conversation with foreigners when I come across with them on the street. I can experience Carnival in "Dreaming Land" near my hometown. I can also watch the newly-released foreign movies in cinemas. Gradually, I feel contented.

Perhaps going to America is really like a dream. One day during summer vacation, after I had just talked on phone with a friend, my teacher called, inquiring about my scores of all possible English proficiency tests I had ever taken, like CET4 (College English Test Band 4), final English exams and college entrance exam, etc. Hearing my answer, he said, "Our college has an opportunity for students to study in America for one year. Call me within ten minutes if you decide to go and come at 2 p. m. for an interview in Foreign Language College building." Later, I passed the first interview as well as a call-back interview and then became a member of China 150 and embarked on my dream journey in America.

After my arrival in America, everything seemed new and strange. I was assigned to Herkimer County Community College. With clean and tidy streets, fresh air, blue sky and delicate villas appearing only in fair tales, Herkimer left me a great impression. During the first few days, our schedule was tightly arranged by teachers of International Office. We went to waterpark, visited baseball museum, watched an opera, went swimming at a professor's pool, and had BBQ, etc. We were busy having fun together. A dozen hours' flight traded me a completely new environment with a huge impact on my way of thinking. Though quite confident about my English, I was startled to find that a real-life conversation with Americans was not easy. I couldn't understand what they said and they also found my spoken English unclear. We could only guess each other's meanings. Having watched lots of American movies and entertainment shows, I thought I should know American culture well, but I found what I had known was far from enough when I was actually in the setting.

August 2008, with my teachers and classmate

Curriculum system in American colleges is rather flexible. There are even no optional or compulsory courses (unless you want to transfer to another college, in which case, common courses should be selected so credit can be transferred). My courses and curriculum are decided by my own interests and needs. During classes, the atmosphere was quite relaxing with a few students in each classroom. The professors were humorous and willing to answer any questions we proposed. There wasn't much homework except for projects. The professors would assign those projects to us nearly two weeks before deadlines. As soon as I was assigned the homework, I thought it was still early and postponed it until later. But as the deadline approached, I found myself facing so many materials to be researched and organized. Rushing to meet the deadlines was painful and caused anxiety. Therefore, we should cultivate a good habit of previewing courses as well as finishing projects in good time. One thing that surprised me was that America, viewed as a country stressing quality education, is actually more "test-oriented" than China. We had several quizzes each week and a few tests a couple of weeks. Nobody would risk slacking off and we had to master all main points in each lecture. In China, on the contrary, we could cram for exams. My major was marketing, so I chose a majority of economics and management courses, such as International Economics and Trade, Marketing, Accounting, Macro Economics, Business Administration, etc. Though I had learned most of the courses in China, I still managed to learn some new things, for the professors gave profoundly interesting lectures, complementing with a few interesting experiences of his own. Besides, the textbooks were updated with latest cases and ideas. In addition, they also offered a variety of meaningful courses like Public Speaking, Golf, American Culture, etc. After I studied Public Speaking, I knew how to organize a presentation and the ever-shy person like me could deliver a public speech with much confidence. American Culture was one of my favorites, for it was flexible with different activities, such as watching a movie, visiting a museum, making Jack-o'-Lanterns, preparing Christmas gifts, etc. Our teacher said we would really appreciate American culture in the course of having fun and trivial daily matters. Tutors in Academic Center provided us with assistance both in our study and language learning. They were all very nice, especially those English-as-a-foreign-Language teachers who were both our teachers and friends.

Janna, Zec, Tack and other China 150 students

As for life in America, the first thing that comes to my mind is food and losing weight. Fast food chains are found everywhere in America— McDonald, KFC, Pizza Hut, etc. For us who are used to rice and vegetables, those heavy, sweet food like hamburgers, pizza, cakes and pasta added to our weight unknowingly. One boy gained ten kilograms within a month. Hearing this, all the girls embarked on their long road of weightlosing. We went running in the gym, swimming in the stadium and joined mountain climbing clubs. We eleven students assigned to this community college and a local Chinese student lived in two big old wooden houses. Each house has a kitchen and two bathrooms, one upstairs, the other downstairs. We each had our own room. During the weekends, we used to buy some vegetables and fruits from Wal-Mart and cook some Chinese dishes as rewards to ourselves. A delight for me was that we didn't bother washing our clothes by hands, but we had to watch out our clothes in case they might shrink after drying. Public transport here was not well-linked, with very few buses, for local people have their own cars. During winter, as it was snowing hard, we had to wrap ourselves up warm to shop in Wal-Mart. When our cheeks were flushed with chilly winds, I missed my own country, and my hometown.

As for interpersonal relationship, Americans value individualism. Unlike students in China who always walk together with their friends on campus, students in America are often seen walking alone, carrying textbooks in their arms, and bags on their backs. There was no class as a group. Students choosing the same courses were classmates. Chinese establish friendship through chatting and sharing while Americans through working together, like attending lectures, discussing assignments, working out, joining clubs, going to parties, etc. Apart from Chinese students, there were also international students from other Asian countries like Japan, Korea, Vietnam and Singapore. With similar culture backgrounds, we became friends soon.

Let me say a few words about the professors. The professor teaching Public Speech always invited us to her house and asked us about recent interesting stories happened to us, and she also shared with us her own funny stories. She said she was like our mother. I remember one day when the four of us international students were giving speeches in AARP, I ran into Professor Mason, my professor of International Trade the semester before. He was supposed to be on vacation in Florida, but he showed up there and greeted me. We had a small chat before it was my turn to give the speech. Standing on the platform, I was nervous, until I saw Mason smiling at me in the audience. I suddenly felt at ease. After the speech we chatted with him happily and bid farewell to him in a hurry. Mason gave me a big hug, telling me that he had driven all the way to meet us after he had read in the local newspaper that some of us took part in voluntary work. Hearing his words, my eyes were welled with tears. The stern-looking Mason who always joked "there is no friendship in business" was so nice. He said, "Remember to call me or send me an

e-mail. We can go and have a cup of coffee before you leave for home and my trip to Israel. " At that moment, I suddenly felt that maybe I would be reluctant to leave the beautiful scenery, kind people here when I had to go.

Though the trip to America to pursue my dream was full of hardships, I gained a lot. I learned up-to-date knowledge and ideas. I travelled with my classmates on our own, learning to face up with difficulties, solve problems independently, tolerate loneliness, arrange my time and find true happiness.

Yuan Yue, from Pengzhou City, Sichuan Province.

I study at Chengdu University of Technology. During my nine months in the US, I studied at Herkimer County Community College.

American Dream

By Qu Mengxi
Southwestern University of Finance and Economics

My father encouraged me to learn English when I was a little girl. Ever since then, a seed of dream has been sowed in my heart, a dream of going to study in America and get to know American culture. To me, CSC-SUNY 150 Program is like a dream. My one-year life in America deepens my understanding of responsibility and gratitude. All hardships and tests have converted into my cherished treasure, lighting up my road ahead.

We were destined to be treated specially, thanks to CSC-SUNY 150, a program aimed to promote Sino-US cultural communication and friendship. We received care and blessing from people from both home and America. As soon as we arrived in New York with our dreams and expectations, we were greeted by people from all walks of societies. Overseas Chinese voluntarily raised funds, held welcome receptions, showering us with warmth from compatriots in a foreign country. The Consulate-General of the People's Republic of China in New York also held a banquet, during which we met with representatives from all colleges. Afterwards, I, together with ten other students, was assigned to study in Herkimer County Community College.

Herkimer is a quiet, peaceful town with slow pace of life. Our college is located on a small hill with a broad view of the whole town. At first I was not accustomed to the quiet life there. I often felt homesick and lonely when I was all by myself. However, as soon as I got busy with my study, life became colorful. I still remember my tension the first time I stepped into the classroom. I was afraid my English might not be good enough for me to understand lectures, but after a few sessions, I found I could understand most part of the lectures, therefore gradually gained confidence. Later, I felt having classes was fun and I could often answer the teachers' questions. I think my way of thinking underwent changes during the one-year study in America. Unconsciously, I no longer translated the English language into Chinese before understanding it. Instead, I think in English, which I benefited a lot.

"International Birthday" Party

As a nation embracing multiple cultures, America set up a platform for us to communicate with the world. In our college, there were overseas students from all over Asia, who became our close friends as we share similar experience abroad. Through learning each other's language and cooking, we exchanged our ideas, learned from each other, and worked hard to fulfill our American dream. In America, each of us had our special birthdays—"International Birthday"—as we called it.

What really touched us were our teachers, as well as lots of other kind and warm-hearted Americans; among them was Durkee, our Public

Speaking teacher. All students of China 150 in this college called her Mom Durkee. She always said, "They are my lovely daughters and sons. " She invited us to her house, cooked meals for us eleven students, allowed us to have her black chocolates, laughed and had fun with us. She was more of our playmate than of our teacher. She was emotional sometimes. Once I chose Wenchuan Earthquake as my speech topic. I had not realized it would be so difficult before the class. When I was giving the speech on the platform, facing attentive classmates with deeply-concerning gaze, as well as Mom Durkee's soothing eyes, I couldn't help shedding tears. Mom Durkee came up to hug me. With wet eyes, she encouraged me to continue. I choked with sobs through the rest of my speech, but all my classmates supported me with their applause, thanking me for sharing with them the unforgetable experience. At that moment, I was deeply moved, realizing that true love was the purest love transcending nations, religions and races. During this year, there were many other Americans who selflessly offered us their warmest care. They spent their festivals together with us to deepen our understanding of their culture. They tutored us our written and spoken English. A teacher called Al said, "My van is your van. " —meaning he would give us a ride whenever we need. True love is selfless. It was they who taught us to be thankful.

The one-year American dream witnessed my growth and alternation to an independent, open-minded person who's always striving to be stronger. With my passion to chase my dream, and eagerness to know more about the country, I travelled with my suitcase. I once slept over on a bench at an air terminal, took a bus at night for eighteen hours of ride, waited at an empty bus stop all alone.... I can not even imagine doing all these before I came here. All these experiences are the most valuable wealth for me.

Youth should have no boundaries but to fly up high with dreams. China 150 is a cherished memory for me. It is radiant with dazzling beam, lighting up my road ahead.

No matter what difficulties life brings to you, remember there is always hope and faith.

Qu Mengxi, from Mianyang City, Sichuan Province.

I study at Southwestern University of Finance and Economics. During my nine months in the US, I studied at Herkimer County Community College, majoring in International Business.

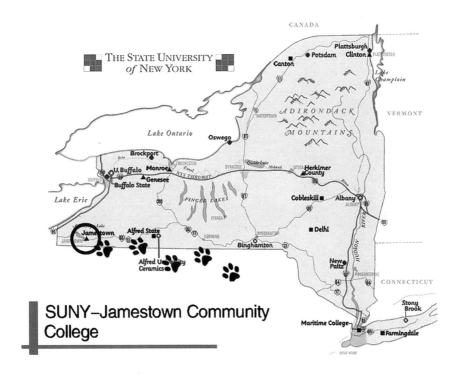

THE STATE UNIVERSITY *of* NEW YORK

CANADA

Plattsburgh
Clinton
Potsdam
Canton

Lake Champlain

VERMONT

ADIRONDACK

Lake Ontario

Oswego

MOUNTAINS

Brockport

Erie

U. Buffalo   Monroe   Genesee   Buffalo State

NYS THRUWAY

ROCHESTER

SYRACUSE

UTICA   Herkimer County

Lake Erie

FINGER LAKES

ITHACA

Cobleskill   Albany

Jamestown   Alfred State

Alfred University Ceramics

Binghamton   Delhi

New Paltz

POUGHKEEPSIE

CONNECTICUT

Stony Brook

Maritime College   Farmingdale

NEW YORK

SUNY–Jamestown Community College

Remembrance of Those Days in America

By Wang Lei
University of Electronic Science and Technology of China

It has been nearly two weeks since we came back from studying in America. We have almost adjusted to life here again, while occasionally missing teachers and friends in America. I recall that some classmates interrupted a lecture by raising a hand; I recollect that my roommate Adam drove me to Wal-Mart and Wegmans to buy vegetables and rice... All these people have offered great help to us both academically and domestically, making our lives both fun and easy. In America, I experienced a completely new learning and life style, as well as brand-new culture. From those helpful people, I learned to be ready to help others and always be grateful.

The teachers there are all kind to us. When we first arrived, we had to choose courses, which was a big challenge for us, for we didn't know most of the English names of the courses. Even if we knew, the content might not be the same as we expected. So a professor called Marie Plumb was invited to give us a detailed explanation. She paused every few sentences to make sure we understood her, if not she would explain drawing on the blackboard. Later on, we chose her Physics course and

Before we left, our vice president Marilyn Zagora and her husband Bob invited us to their house again to celebrate our graduation.

found her a good teacher. During her class, she often asked us specifically whether we understood before she continued. I loved her classes, except for too many assignments. Apart from essays for each subject, she demanded us to write a report of several pages. I stayed up all night several times in order to finish the work, which I had never done in China before; therefore, I felt extremely tired. After mid-term exam, she invited the whole class to her house. While in private, she told us it was us that she had really intended to ask for. Unfortunately, we didn't go to her house due to time clash with other engagements. Marilyn, vice president of the college, invited us three times to her house. Her husband Bob and she came to pick us up every time, cooked us delicious food and brewed Chinese Longjing tea for us. On the day we left the college, she came to see us off at 6 a.m. after nearly an hour's drive from her house to college. The day before we left America, she went to the Consulate-General to bid farewell to us.

Before coming to America, I didn't know there was Community College. Later on I found that in such a college there were lots of benefits for students. The college I was at, Jamestown Community College, for example, has a Main Street where tutoring was offered to students free of charge. All students of this college can apply for tutoring. I often went to a test room and got familiar with Kaye Young, the lady in charge. Whenever I had any questions, she would explain to me patiently or direct me to someone in charge if she could not solve my problems. Other teachers were patient as well.

On commencement day, Kaye Young and I took a picture outside of the school gym.

They wouldn't be upset even if they were interrupted in class. Later on our college held a badminton competition for the staff. Kaye asked me to be her partner. The first few games were easy, but the competition gradually became tougher as we engaged more spectators. But it was a pity we didn't win first in the end.

Another teacher is Catherine. Her husband, a Russian called Anton also teaches in our college. None of us were in his class, but he came to us and took us to Cleveland. We spent Thanksgiving with their family. An interesting thing happened to me. I seldom have birthday parties and very few classmates know when my birthday is. During our trip to Cleveland, Catherine happened to find out I had my birthday a few days ago without a party showed to me by my Chinese friends. She whispered to me on our way back that she would make it up for me in a fancy restaurant downtown. I thought she was just being nice and would forget about it. The next day, however, she sent me an e-mail asking about my convenient time slot so she could make a reservation. Later on, she and Anton picked me up and we had dinner together. I ordered genuine American Steak. After dinner, we watched Christmas Parade. Although it was a make-up birthday, I found it the happiest one I'd ever had.

I became good friends with other Americans as well. My roommate Adam is a great American guy, chubby and lovely (though he doesn't like to be described as lovely). The first time we met, he found we had no TV set, so he moved his own into the living room for us to watch. He also took two others from his house and lent them to my friends. As we had no transport tools, he promised to drive us to shopping every week. In the first semester, he said he would take me to his home when my English improved. He really kept his words and introduced me to his mother, brother and grandparents. I remember clearly that two days before our departure, he invited us to his party. On our way back, he suddenly called out my name and gave me a big hug, saying "We are friends forever."

One of my classmates Alaina is also a nice girl. At our Drawing class, I always asked her when I didn't understand the teacher's words well.

When we learned to draw people, she proposed to be my model. Once I asked her about where to find a Bible and how much each one was, for a friend of mine asked me to buy one for him. As the price exceeded his budget, I decided not to buy one. However, when I came back to class for next session, Alaina took her Bible from her bag and offered me as a gift. I was much surprised as I didn't expect her to be so considerate.

There are many other people accompanying us through the past nine months, during which we had much fun though sometimes being exhausted from study. We were reluctant to leave and most of my classmates shed tears at the Consulate-General on departure.

With my friend Ben and his family on Christmas Day

Thank you! Truly, thank you all!

I learned a lot from the experience in the USA. I will treasure the friendship with my American friends for all my life. My thanks go to everybody who has helped us!

Wang Lei, from Pengzhou City, Sichuan Province.

I study at University of Electronic Science and Technology of China. During my nine months in the US, I studied at SUNY – Jamestown Community College. I like playing all kinds of ball games, such as soccer and ping-pong as well as listening to music and watching movies.

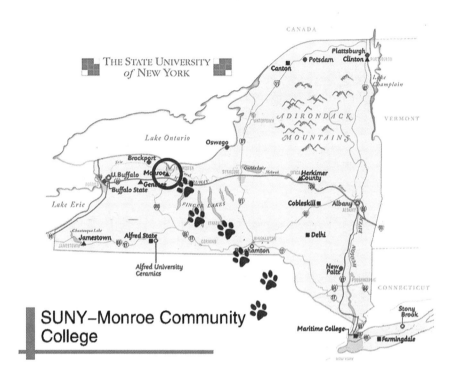

SUNY–Monroe Community
College

Our American Moms

By Li Xiaodan
China West Normal University

When the plane took off, I recalled the moment nine months ago when the plane had touched down and I set foot on the soil of the United States of America. Time passed away insensibly and it seemed that everything happened yesterday. I gazed into the sky and bade farewell to this land, where I had lived for nearly one year, and gave my best regards to my friends and American Moms. When I first arrived in US, Mom always told me to call every week, because she would always be worried about my life and study in US. As time went by she was more at ease, for she knew that there were many Moms taking care of me in US.

Suzanne Elrayess

When we were still in China, Suzanne, an English teacher, got into contact with us by e-mail. She not only told us about her family, but also sent us her photos. She said that she had spent one year in Hangzhou, China at the age of three and that her younger brother was born in Hangzhou. Because of her, her whole family is inextricably associated with China. As the dean of ESL, Suzanne was looking forward to our arrival.

On the day when we arrived at Monroe Community College, Suzanne couldn't wait to meet us. We embraced and she carefully helped us choose autumn courses. Without doubt, we selected her ESL201. She paid special attention to us in class. The most moving thing was that she took us out for a walk almost every weekend. Suzanne was never a woman with feigned emotions, because she always helped us practically in action. During the days before our leaving, she sent us e-mails every day to ask what we still needed and where we hadn't been to. She said she wanted us to remember Rochester and Monroe Community College and that she loved us. Two days before we left Monroe Community College, we still hadn't got a school banner. In order to help us find a school

From left to right: Li Xiaodan, Suzanne Elrayess, Wei Lin, Xie Yue, Zhou Chenchen

banner, she accompanied us on our search for two hours on the campus, asking for it for us. We followed her and didn't know how to thank her for the help. Later in the afternoon, she called and told us that a banner had been found and asked us to go to her office. When we entered the office, she said, with tears in her eyes: "I know that this is the last time for us to see each other." Saying these words, she kept wiping her moist eyes: "This is embarrassing. I have too many tears. Please don't mind it. I love you. My kids are not with me, and you have accompanied me like my kids. Thank you very much for the pleasure you've brought to us." We hugged and wept.

She is one of our American Moms. She said that she would remain in the college, send us e-mails and come to China if there was any opportunity. She usually said jokingly that she was old and fat and that there was certainly not enough space for her in China. And we smiled and replied that there would be space for her whenever she paid a visit to China.

Janet Glocker

Janet was Vice President of Monroe Community College. She was in charge of teaching affairs. She often asked what we needed, and invited us to her home for dinner. She gave us presents whenever a festival fell.

During the Spring Festival of the traditional Chinese Lunar Calendar, she invited us to her home to prepare a Chinese-style meal. The Chancellor also came. We had a very good time that night. We sat around the table, on which traditional Chinese-style cuisine was served, and enjoyed the meal till almost midnight as if we were family members. A weekend before our leaving, Janet invited us to have a barbecue at her home and we spent a very pleasant early summer evening. When she escorted us to the dormitory gate we hugged tightly and her eyes were wet. She said that she would miss us and then turned around and left. That evening, I opened the e-mail and her affectionate words popped up. I couldn't resist crying. Each of her e-mails began with "My dear Chinese daughters" and ended with "Love, your American Mom."

Celebrating Chinese New Year at Janet Glocker's home

Susan Salvador

Susan was also a Vice President of the college. She was in charge of student affairs, like boarding. She was a brilliant and energetic woman, with affectionate words. She not only held a graduation evening ceremony for us, but also planted a tree on the campus at midday on May 12. She said that the root of the tree would pierce down deep into the earth and our future life would be steady and solid, just as the tree was deeply rooted in the earth. She hoped that we would forever grow vigorously just like the tree we had planted.

In China we have our Moms who love us very much, and in America there are also many Moms who love us very much. We will remember and cherish the help they have provided for us. During the nine months in US, they regarded us as their own kids and we enjoyed and got accustomed to their maternal love.

We got to know our American Moms on our way of life, and we wish them all the best.

Our graduation celebration at Susan's home

Maybe I am not the best one, but I do believe I am one of the best.

Li Xiaodan, from Dujiangyan City, Sichuan Province.

I study Teaching Chinese as a Second Language at China West Normal University. In America, I studied at SUNY – Monroe Community College.

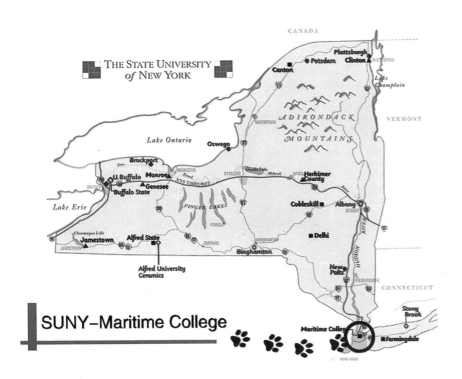

THE STATE UNIVERSITY
of NEW YORK

SUNY–Maritime College

Mind to Mind Contact

By Fang Dongsheng
China West Normal University

Nine months' trip, nine months' of growing. With all sorts of feelings, now I'm writing this article in Wenchuan County, all the scenes of those nine months are still vivid in my mind. It's hard for me to look back on the tragic scene of May 12, 2009. During the quake the house of my family collapsed and my parents were blocked in Wenchuan County. I rented a small apartment in Chengdu with another student who had the same situation as me; we encouraged and consoled each other. In order to divert our attention, both of us decided to look for a language training center in Chengdu to learn oral English. In order to find a language center with

At Professor Eric's home on Christmas with my French friend

reasonable prices and high teaching quality, both of us went to various training institutions or centers to consult and take tests every day. We didn't realize that all of these efforts would yield fruit in later interviews. Actually, after my class teacher had told me to go back to my university for an English interview, I succeeded in a series of interviews and luckily became a member of China 150.

I was curious about everything when I just arrived in the United

States of America. I still remember how excited I was to attend my first class. Though I could not fully understand what the teacher was saying, I was still very happy. Before I came here, I had watched some American movies. At that time I thought that study was so easy for American students, but little by little, I found that the universities in the USA were quite different from what I had thought. I can say that there are big differences. I completely realized the preciseness of teaching in American universities—homework, mid-term exams, final exams and final thesis, none of them can be overlooked. Really I was thrown off to my feet by tiredness. A sudden transfer from a Chinese environment to listening to courses in English, reading and doing homework in English—this new life wasn't a small challenge; but little by little, I found more pleasure, more joys.

Celebrating Mid-Autumn Festival with George Hu, Assistant to the Governor of New York State

Since we joined the class in the middle of the course and studied with American students, we had lots of opportunities to communicate with them, and we could get to know their opinions and thoughts, which was really great. Attending classes in American universities, you'll find there is a case behind each theory. For example, each time while the teacher was teaching about macroeconomic regulation, he would talk about the financial rescue strategy of the American Government. For the first semester of the junior year, I chose the course of English Literature. I began to read English poems, and Shakespeare's play *Othello*. For a science major student, this was a brand-new experience. After attending this course, I tried to read the original English version of some novels, such as *Into the Wild*, and I found it really fantastic! Office hours once or twice a week for the students to meet the professors is also a wonderful opportunity which can't be missed. You can have the chance to communicate face to face, one to one with professors with different backgrounds who have either graduated from Columbia University or have ever worked in Wall Street. Topics were not restricted in office hours. We could talk about anything. Once I talked with the Professor about topics ranging from national problems to buying discounted goods. I felt that the Professor was so close to us, as the Professor said: "Our job is to help you."

SUNY − New York Maritime College is one of the few specialised maritime colleges in the USA. Two courses gave me profound impression— Shipping Management and Marine Insurance. Simply speaking, Shipping Management talks about the classification of all types of ships, the constitution of ships and ships management. While Marine Insurance discusses insurance for ships, focusing on corresponding legal texts. These two courses brought me to the unknown sea world, mysterious and fanciful, which fascinated me a lot. The college also offered special lectures on pirates, which were very interesting.

I want to mention one very small detail. At the end of the last Economics class, the professor stood voluntarily at the classroom door and shook hands with every student, expressing his thanks for the students' cooperation and support, and handing out leaflets on the courses he was going to teach the next semester. This professor put himself in a position equal to that of the students', making us feel very close to him. This impressed me very much.

I have to mention the deep friendship with my American teachers and classmates. I was so touched by my professor, Eric, who voluntarily gave us an oral English class every week. Our talks ranged from English pronunciation to American history, from American football to Chinese "Xiaolong Baozi." We chatted with each other without reserve, and had a pleasant Christmas in his house. I was touched by my classmate Paul who took us to experience different aspects of American life, with our happy laughter left in the New Jersey Amusement Park. I also appreciated Chen

Bin, a Chinese student who took us to Princeton University, Yale University to experience the unusual charm of such top universities...

Maybe because I got used to American life, I felt time flying in the second semester of Junior 2. Without my consciousness, the nine months' American life thus ended. If I'm asked about some special profound feeling, I think that I deeply feel a kind of responsibility, a kind of

Watching a show in New Jersey with Paul

responsibility which is much heavier than that of people of my age: the great trust by people from my hometown and the expectations of my motherland. I hope that we will live up to all the expectations. We will surely do something in a down-to-earth way. I still remember the first gathering for Mid-Autumn Festival in the USA. We couldn't help weeping when we saw pictures of the Wenchuan Earthquake which is forever a pain in our minds that can't be touched. However, in my mind, the future of my hometown will be bright and splendid!

Treasure what you have now.

Fang Dongsheng, from Wenchuan County, Sichuan Province.

I study International Business and Trade at China West Normal University. In America, I studied International Business and Trade at SUNY – Maritime College.

THE STATE UNIVERSITY
of NEW YORK

SUNY–New Paltz

Two Diaries Written in the United States of America

By Tang Xinglin
Sichuan Normal University

Diary One: Yesterday, Today and Tomorrow

Yesterday

Yesterday was December 20, 2008, the first day of the winter vacation. The snow fall was heavy and deep enough to sink in. It was a white world all around. The squirrels had already prepared their winter food. We couldn't see their busy traces now. There were several unknown birds flying in the woodland, which shook off the snow. I took my newly bought camera, intending to record this peaceful world of snow. The pines might be the most stubborn trees in this season, which didn't change their green appearance. Thick snow weighed down on the leaves and branches, making the pines look very special. Where I walked there were just my own footprints. The snow was very thick. I walked with difficulty, but my route was very straight.

In the former days there were Australian geese swimming on the lake and sometimes there was naughty fish jumping out of water, and a series of rips were dispersed and disappeared. Then the lake surface was iced over. I guess the geese couldn't stand on the surface, so they migrated. Fish were restricted by the ice. Now the lake was covered with heavy snow, a white world all over. Two weeping willows across the lake stood lonely expecting the arrival of spring. Fortunately, they were accompanied by the benches.

The farmer's happy family

In the evening I went as a guest to a farmer's for a Christmas party. It's a very harmonious and happy family. The family members were sitting around together, eating all sorts of snacks, playing the guitar, shaking all sorts of bells, singing Christmas songs. Both the grown-ups and the children were very cheerful. Vici (a warm-hearted community member) picked Leo (a roommate of mine, another Chinese student) and me up back and forth. I was very lucky. From the people I met and the things I heard about, I was feeling the differences between American and Chinese cultures.

Today

Today is the Winter Solstice in China. We don't have the custom of eating dumplings on this special day in my hometown. But I haven't made dumplings myself for a long time, so I decide to have a try. I got up very early, making dough in the kitchen, unfreezing chopped meat, chopping onions and leeks...

The cooking skill that I had learned from my mom was helpful

All Chinese students at NP were full of love and like a big family. We made dumplings by ourselves on Winter Solstice.

this day, but I had never tried to flatten the dough to make wrappers of round shapes. Today it was my first time to make wrappers. Finally we had wrappers of all shapes for making dumplings. Everyone was busy, helping with the cooking. The final result was good. We ate very cheerfully.

Tomorrow

Tomorrow I'll go to work. I got a campus job for the winter

vacation. It's very complicated here to get a job. First you need to apply for the job. If the boss agrees, he'll give you a letter. Then you take this letter and your passport to apply for a social security number. Only after getting a social security number can you work legally and make money. Generally speaking, international students are not allowed to work off campus during study periods. Anyway this job wasn't easy for me to get. Although the salary is the lowest in New York State— $ 7. 15 per hour, and I can work no more than twenty hours per week, I feel it's not too bad. I'll work hard to make money.

Diary Two: Buffalo Trip during Spring Break

We are having spring break these days. Several days ago, I was very happy to receive the good news of attending a training project in Buffalo. On Friday morning after the English exam, I rushed to a small town— Poughkeepsie on another side of Hudson River. When I got off the bus, I found I was at a small railway station, simple but not lacking modern amenities. I fished out $ 1. 5 to buy a bottle of water, and then I sat on the cold bench to wait for the train to approach. The outside of the train seemed very old; it hadn't been painted for a long time. But the interior was completely facilitated, even with access to wireless network. Unfortunately, I struggled for four hours in vain—I couldn't get connected. I just depended on several songs from the hard disk of my PC to pass the six hours on the trip.

Outside the train the sun was still shining. Maybe as I'm used to the simplicity of Train K390 from Chengdu to Fuzhou, this kind of comfortable seat made me feel sick. I felt dizzy and the sunshine was too bright for my eyes. I changed to the aisle seats frequently. There were less than ten passengers in the compartment (most of them were on short trips and got off the way). I was in a daze and fell asleep. I didn't know how long later when I heard some announcements. I woke up and didn't dare to fall asleep again. My eyes were staring at the rails on the sleepers. Fifty minutes later, I set foot on the land called "Buffalo" which was said to be

flattened by buffalos' feet. Walking out of the station, I found the sunshine still dazzling. The sky was very blue. Standing for several minutes in the gentle breeze, I felt cold. Buffalo is a small city in the north of New York State, which borders Canada. Though it was mid March, the accumulated snow wasn't all melted. It was flat all around, with no hills in view. There isn't too much cultivated land, and the farms are very centralized. In the evening I was interviewed by two journalists. Over dinner I talked with them about some funny things they came across in China. I could feel that they loved Chinese culture very much. I accepted their interview without hesitation. The topics were about what I had seen here, what I had heard here, and how I had felt here, and about my study experience and life adaptation process after I was assigned to a campus alone. The whole interview lasted about thirty minutes. Since the train trip took me more than six hours, I was very tired. But I kept smiling till the end of the interview. I think generally speaking big potatoes wouldn't accept an interview in this kind of situation. For me, I'm just like a grain of sand in the desert and a drop of water in the sea. This kind of honor isn't easy to get. How could I reject? I didn't know what I had said in front of the camera while I was dizzy and sleepy. In the end when I was asked to sign on a piece of paper, I couldn't keep my hand shaking whilst holding the pen.

That night, I didn't feel sleepy even after midnight. I began to chat with my roommate, about life and ideals. We mainly talked about each other's study and life for more than an hour, feeling very affectionate. Then I walked into the bathroom, turned on the shower and washed away that day's tiredness. It was already 10:30 in the morning the next day when I got up. I'd slept for almost ten hours. The activity began at 11:40 a. m. I bought a cup of coffee, and a slice of Apple Turnover (similar to apple pie) in a hurry in the Student Union Building. After gulping the food, I rushed to the library meeting room. I ran inside without registering. I was very excited as I saw one of my "group members"(a student from the same university as me in China), as ever. The whole activity didn't start until 12:30 p. m., to be exact. After an official welcome speech and an introduction of VIPs, we started a brain storming game. All of us were divided in eight small groups. Each group had the same number of toothpicks, a plastic straw, one disposable paper cup plus a bottle of mousse. The aim was to see which group could make the highest "model" within the limited time. The model of our group was 48 cm. Every one was happy. This was really a process of cooperation. All in all, I felt that the whole afternoon I was practicing oral English. It was really tiring! The only thing to look forward to was the Chinese food after the activity.

The activity was finally over. Dr. Charles (a leader of Buffalo State College) ended the activity by giving an official speech of thanks. Here the Chinese food was much more delicious than that in China House near our school. After the meal, I went to see Niagara Falls with three girls from Monroe Community College and their teachers. Buffalo State College is not far from there, around thirty minutes' bus ride. I appreciated Audra—a teacher from Monroe Community College—very much as she gave us a lift. The weather was great; I could hear the growl of the waterfall without seeing it. Opening the car door I saw a bridge connecting two countries, America and Canada. The latter is just 200 meters away. I could only take a look at Canada over the fall!

The river was totally frozen. It was really a big pity that I couldn't take a boat ride on the river to feel the grand vigor of the waterfall.

On March 15, I got up at 10:30 a.m. I didn't have breakfast. After washing up, I went to wait for the No. 32 bus at the gate of the community. It didn't take long for the bus to come! It took more than thirty minutes to get to the mall (a kind of big shopping center usually seen in the USA). I bought two bars of chocolate to supplement my physical strength. I didn't realize that it did work. I rushed crazily to one shop and another. However, at two o'clock in the afternoon I felt extremely hungry. Then I chose a Chinese fast food restaurant in the mall. The fried shrimps made by the cook were really tasty, and very cheap; the dishes were very delicious. After eating, I continued to walk in Macy Shopping Center for two hours. I didn't get anything in the end. The

items I fancied were too expensive for me to afford while those that I could afford were not satisfactory at all. This is how I felt when I was shopping at Macy's.

It was already 5 p. m. when I got to Buffalo State College. One friend had told me that there was a Chinese market nearby. I couldn't help going there to buy several bottles of spicy sauce. I knew I would be satisfied even with preserved Sichuan pickles. The sunshine was still dazzling. I sat at a bus station to wait for the bus. After about half an hour, the No. 20 bus finally arrived. I asked the driver about the Chinese market, but he didn't have any idea. So I had to get on the bus anyway.

I dropped $2 into the bus fare box and went to sit down on a back seat with big and small bags in hands. The Bus No. 20 is for downtown. On the way I searched every advertisement panel to see whether there were any Chinese characters on it, or any remarkable sign of Chinese. This kind of search continued till the end of the bus route—to the terminal. The last several passengers gave me a light smile when getting off. Maybe they were wondering, who was this big fool? Yes, I was really stupid. I hurried off the bus without knowing where the place was. But if you never try, how can you know whether you can make it! When I got off, I said again "sadly" to the driver "What a pity! I can't find it. Could you please tell me how to go back?" The driver answered nicely, "Just go across the street. I'll be there soon. " I thought, "I'm really unlucky! The driver earned $4 so easily from me. "

The street was very busy; it seemed there was a kind of parade. Groups of students (around twenty years old, I guess) gathered in front of the bars. They were dressed in green, with green hats on their heads, clover on their faces, and green necklaces around their necks, and green glasses with alcoholic drinks in their hands. I wanted to laugh at first sight. In my country, what serious consequence it will be if women give "green hat" to men! But here it's different. Both men and women wear green hats! It seemed that they were waiting for the coming of spring. March 17 is St. Patrick's Day (the most important festival of American Irish, of course, they won't miss drinking this day) . The policemen are the most stressed under such circumstances; they are afraid that something might happen. So police cars with a clear logo "911" stopped at nearly every block. And the rubbish car was busy. The roads were really dirty. This was my first impression of Buffalo.

March 16, Monday, sunny day! Today is the day when I leave Buffalo. I like there. I like everything except that there is no mountain. Mrs. Blackburn said that she would pick me up to catch the train back to school. Soon after breakfast, she arrived. She is an old lady respected by everyone of Buffalo State College! She devotes all her life to this university and founded a scholarship with her salary and pension. I guess she's around 70 or 80. She arrived in my dormitory—North Wing Hall on time, at 8:30 a.m. On the way, Mrs. Blackburn asked me whether I had a good time in Buffalo and whether everything was okay for me.

At 9:00 a.m., we arrived at the Depew station where three days ago I got off the train. Mrs. Blackburn stopped the car, and asked me to wait a second. I got off the car and hugged her closely, just like hugging with my grandmother (it's a pity that I have never seen my grandmother with my own eyes, and I have never had the chance to hug her like this). Maybe I won't see Mrs. Blackburn again for the rest of my life. I called her my American Grandmother, and she smiled.

It is said that life is a journey on which all the scenes you see, all the people you meet and all the things you see are affecting you and changing you all the time.

Tang Xinglin, from Mianyang City, Sichuan Province.
I study at Sichuan Normal University. In America, I studied at SUNY - New Paltz.

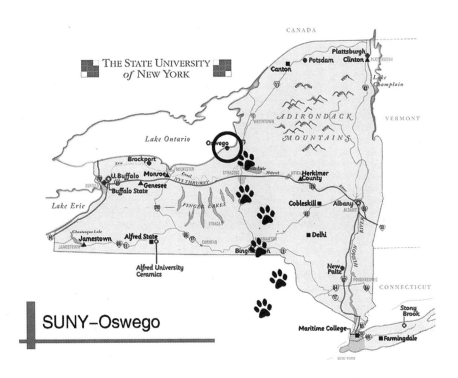

SUNY–Oswego

Nine Months in New York

By Jiang Lili
Sichuan University

During the nine months in New York, I learned to respect and share.

Studying in New York

In New York, a city with multiple cultures, university professors are from all over the world. Under my teacher's guidance, based on rich teaching resources and my professional knowledge, I did a survey around the whole campus. The objective was to study the influence of learning experience of American students on cognition of Chinese culture. This research would have a reference value for the university to establish a specialisation of Chinese Studies. There was a very interesting part, which asked the students to describe China in three words. According to the answers from eighty questionnaires, the three most used words were "traditional, population and strict." "Polite, smart and technologically-advanced" accounted for a considerable proportion. Based on this questionnaire around the school, I finished my paper titled "Learning Experiences and Awareness of China and Chinese Culture" with the help of my tutor, and I had the chance to be invited to participate in the "7 th International Seminar of Chinese for Foreigners" held in Guangxi, China this summer vacation hosted by Yale University. My efforts in study during the whole semester were rewarded.

Working in New York

Students can go to the school's tutoring center to apply for regular tutoring, for free, for a certain course. Teaching assistants (TAs) must be students who have taken this course and have got an A on it, or who are specially authorized by the professor of this course. The tutoring center pays a minimum wage of New York State $7.15 an hour. Since TAs are students themselves, it's much easier for the students to communicate with someone of the same age. Such kind of tutoring is very popular among students. The school has Chinese course, and many students need help. So I applied to the professor of the Chinese course. After an interview, I was selected by the tutoring center among numerous applicants, and I became a Chinese teaching assistant of the school. This semester, I had two students learning Chinese. One was Charles who had attended an exchange course with Zhejiang Gongshang University for one semester and had just come back to USA, a junior in Accounting; the other one was Caroline who intended to go to Beijing for one year study, a sophomore in Anthropology. I was so touched by the extreme passion of these two students for Chinese. At the same time I felt confident about the future of my major, which reinforced my determination to continue in this specialisation.

Shows in New York

I learned to play the *erhu* in my childhood, and I was deeply engrossed with Chinese traditional music. In New York, owing to *erhu*, I made a lot of friends. One enthusiastic tune named "Horse Racing" filled my American friends with curiosity about the instrument of two strings from the East. American students bought *erhus* online and asked me to be their teacher. Then I offered free *erhu* classes from 7 to 10 p.m. each Friday evening which really attracted many people. Now my students can play many simple songs by *erhu*.

Owing to my passion for Chinese traditional music, I was hired as the only international student program emcee by the school radio station. I played Chinese traditional music in each program, and it was warmly welcomed by the local audiences. Besides, I was invited to give performances at the Chinese New Year Evening Party and Asia Culture Exposition Closing Ceremony in Columbia University and Princeton University of Ivy League.

I was invited by Columbia University in Chinese Spring Festival on February 5, 2009.

Walking in New York

The school's vacation provides many outgoing opportunities for students. I went to Boston, Massachusetts using my earned salary to see Harvard University and MIT. Walking again on the road of freedom, I felt the young American history. I had been to New York City several times. The Statue of Liberty holds highly the torch of victory; the skating rink of Rockefeller Center is still full of people; in front of the building of U. N. the national flag of China is flying high. The peace of Central Park, the flourishing of the exhibits of Metropolitan Museum, the depression of Wall Street, the foreign tourists with cameras in Times Square and the pity of not having appropriate opportunity to enjoy an opera, etc. —all these

Recording in the radio station

things opened my view, and I felt the real sense of the Chinese saying "Read ten thousand books, travel ten thousand miles. "

Growing up in New York

What's more, I spent the most special Chinese New Year in New York—I met Yao Ming on the first day of the New Year. Since Yao Foundation was planning to donate primary schools to Sichuan earthquake-stricken area, what we could do was to make suggestions to Yao Ming. We told Yao Ming that we didn't come for his autograph.

A gift ("Mianzhu New Year Painting") to Yao Ming on Feb. 6, 2009

We wanted a very meaningful New Year present—to establish China 150 Volunteer Team. We wanted the support of "Yao Foundation." We asked him to consider the sites of the Hope Primary Schools in Shifang, Deyang, Jiangyou and Mianyang, because they didn't have close social concern. We told Yao Ming that the Mianzhu New Year Painting needed

Our Oswego Crew

to be succeeded to younger generations, and the ethnic cultures of Qiang and Zang needed to be passed on. So, we hoped that the Hope Primary Schools founded by Yao Foundation would provided such special courses. Yao Ming was very happy. He and his fund managers promised to

258

cooperate with China 150. When I presented the Mianzhu New Year Painting to Yao Ming on behalf of my group, I got a "high" hug. Yao Ming is really very very tall. But everyone says that his wisdom is much taller than his height.

At this point of writing, I let out a sigh of relief. During the nine months, I changed from being lacking in knowledge to being kind of confident. I'm grateful to all the people who care about our growing-up. We have learned how to be grateful. Being grateful doesn't mean paying debts. It means living well, showing respect, and sharing with others. Being grateful also means taking responsibilities. When you learn to take responsibilities, you understand what's called growing-up.

As soon as you learn to be grateful, you will get to understand respect and sharing; as soon as you learn how to respect and share, you will come to understand how to be responsible; as soon as you will learn to be responsible, you learn the meaning of being mature—Thank you for the trip to America which makes me feel the growing-up.

Jiang Lili, from Deyang City, Sichuan Province.

I study Teaching Chinese as a Second Language at Sichuan University. During my nine months in the US, I studied at SUNY－Oswego, majoring in Chinese Education.

Facing the Sea with Love and Happiness
—For My Short but Unforgettable Stay in the USA

By Tu Meng

Southwestern University of Finance and Economics

If I were asked to summarize my days in USA in one phrase, I'd say "painful but happy."

I haven't recalled my first few days in the USA for really a long time, until today, until there is once again radiant sunshine after more than 200 days of my stay, during which all of us spent a winter full of snowstorms. I remember that the sunsets now are still as glorious as the ones when I first arrived. I faced the sea and waited for the days with spring blossoms. Now I still remember that as the days drew near to going back home, I felt more and more homesick until I was in the Consulate-General of the People's Republic of China in New York, where I was weeping, reluctant to part. I suddenly found that I had accumulated such profound emotion in the short nine months. Never was I so aching to go back home as then, even though I knew that one day in the future I would miss here a lot. I think I can say that I finally painstakingly finished this tour, sitting beside the window through which the last of the afternoon sunshine flooded, turning the pages of the worn-out diaries, recalling those days, those persons and those things in those days.

The moment we arrived back in my country, even if it was a long and tiring journey, our joy and excitement couldn't be covered up. Our mobile phones were continuously receiving text messages of "Welcome home." At that moment, I really wanted to weep. At the very moment the plane landed, I just wanted to say: Chengdu, my hometown, we're back! One year's experience gives me too many stories to share.

Sometimes I turn over the photos which had been taken before I came to the USA, recalling the babyish smile at that time. Even I, myself, am surprised at my changes. The two short semesters, for me, were as long as two years. Suddenly I remember the speech I heard on my first day in the USA. The speaker said: "Your life in the USA will be like a function, with high tides and low ebbs, ups and downs, and it will finally be inclined to be flat." I didn't fully understand his speech until today. I grew up in such a process.

I delayed in writing this article. There are too many things to write about. I don't know where to begin. Please allow me to begin the story by quoting my Mother's words, the real portraits of my life in the USA: abandon bravely, go on with passion.

The other day while I was tidying my drawers, I sorted out nearly one

In March, 2009, I went to an economics research conference held by Federal Reserve Bank of Dallas.

hundred papers written by me in the nine months. There were about ten thick books on the table; each page of which read and noted in just nine months. I know clearly that I haven't written so numerous articles in the past twenty years as in the past year, nor read so many books. In the eyes of the Americans, Chinese students are robots; eight or nine out of ten students with high scores are Chinese students. But please believe that it's not because the courses in the USA are very simple, nor because Chinese kids are more intelligent, but because we read those books page by page, sometimes more than once. Our diligence deserved high scores. Studying here was by no means easy—6 courses and forty-two exams for the whole semester, six team projects, six class presentations, and homework of six courses. My roommates and I never slept before two o'clock in the morning. I am not exaggerating here, since this was my actual experience. It seemed that I had gone back to my high school life in

China. But such great efforts would be rewarded. When you get the highest score in the class, when the professor acknowledges you, when your team members say thanks to you, you will put on a smile and your eyes will be wet.

I have to admit that American higher education seems to have adopted China's exam system. Though it's hard, I gained a lot in repeated reading and practicing. There were around twenty students in the class of my specialty. We had many opportunities to communicate with the professors. And we had a lot of extracurricular activities, too. It took a great deal of time to prepare for the paper, though. We could try many things, though not necessarily being able to succeed, I never gave up any opportunity to approach success. In the last ten days of March, I went to Dallas in Texas to attend an economic forum. Without an especially solid economic foundation, without taking a course of Statistical Economics, I spent three days making the model that I would discuss and making practical proposals. When I finished my five minutes' presentation with a clear mind, the meeting emcee (MC, Master of Ceremony) came over to me and said: "You're the most excellent presentation representative today. " At that moment, I only wanted to hug her to express my thanks. I gained her recognition not because my point of view was astute, but because of my diligent attitude towards this forum. In many cases in the USA, attitude determines final result. These influential activities show the superiority of American education over that of ours, but American education is not perfect. Maybe many students in China have high expectations on American team projects as I used to. But when I was in the States I missed the team projects back in China where though each time we have to search for directions ourselves, we know how to benefit from mutual discussion. With American kids, the case was different. In team projects they just put together each other's part. Thus the team project loses its real meaning. However, in each team project we worked with people of different personalities—diligent, lazy, irresponsible…All in all, it was not easy to cooperate with them, but I learned to get along with different people. Actually, this one year's study gradually guided me to the world stage. In

August I'll fly to Seoul, Korea, to participate in a Harvard Project on Asian and International Relations and give a presentation.

This kind of opportunity gives me the chance to experience different people, different things and different scenes in the world. The noise of New York, the academic atmosphere in Boston, the magnificence of Niagara Falls, the fairy tale world of Okara, the radiant sunshine of California, and the peace of Dallas... I went on a long journey every one and a half months; I began to love this kind of life. I compensated myself by taking an appropriate journey and rest after each effort. When I returned I began to continue to study and work. In each outing, whatever hotels, air tickets, and scenic places, I tried to practice my capacity to deal with every occurrence. Now I can be a guide myself.

Without noticing, I have written quite a lot. Actually these are only part of the stories. Talking with the professors, playing games, drawing pictures and designing advertisements with American kids, these are the parts to be memorized. I still remember that before my leaving, my professor of Oil Painting said to me, "You are talented. No matter how busy you are, no matter who says you are wrong, don't give up and keep doing your paintings." When I was criticized by my fellows, I made an effort to compensate my mistakes; when misunderstood, I tried to explain; when unfairly treated, I was brave enough to fight.... These are the parts which helped me grow up. This one year is the year when I had the most tears and sweat. The joys, sorrows, ups and downs are worth recalling. Without the experiences and lessons, there wouldn't be today's smiles. America is realistic. It has taught us how to survive. When we have to experience difficulties, it's not a solution to recall or to weep with the door shut. The solution is to pack up your tears, stand up bravely to fight.

All the children of China 150 were studying in New York State. Though we were far away from each other, and didn't have many chances to get together, we seemed to know each other very well because of China 150. We were in different places, having different stories, each of which must be brilliant. All in all, we tried our best to have a good time in this year. This year, I began to get new knowledge about the USA—a country standing at the top of the world, about China—a country which draws the world's attention. I realised I was so in love with the land which had given birth to me and nourished me, so in love with the culture and the people here. For many times I dreamed of walking with my family, dreaming of the streets and roads of my hometown. When I saw the kind messages from my mother and my friends, I wept alone in front of the computer. Besides my study, the one year's experience made us understand the road to take and the things to do. I was so eager to go back to the hugs of my relatives, to my familiar places; I missed so much my fellows in "Navigation Plan" of Southwestern University of Finance and Economics, my fellows and pals at the starting point. The day to go back to China was finally approaching. I would go back with love and missing, with achievements to share with my family and friends....

At this moment, when I close my eyes, the figure of Oswego and the familiar light tower will show up. By the bank of the peaceful Lake Ontario, I felt I was facing the sea with love and happiness. This feeling will accompany me all my life.

To us, the past one year was unusual. We learned to be tolerant,grateful, independent and perseverant. With these precious gifts, we will be blossoming on the road ahead.

Tu Meng, from Aba Tibetan and Qiang Autonomous Prefecture, Sichuan Province.
I study at Southwestern University of Finance and Economics. During my nine months in the US, I studied at SUNY − Oswego.

SUNY–Plattsburgh

A True "Flight"

By He Juan
Chengdu University of Technology

"Excitement" lingered on my face ever since that morning of Aug. 15, 2008. Not until I disembarked the plane at JFK International Airport and stepped on the American land did I believe that everything was real, including the one month's preparation for this trip.

It's really incredible that I have really experienced it: one year's study in the USA, which I could not have ever dreamed of.

Upon my arrival in this country, I realized many differences between China and the USA, especially the views-conscientiously mowed lawns which look very tidy and pleasing, tempting one to lie down and have a colorful dream; short but unusually fascinating trees, and the blue sky which we all said too blue to be true, even brighter than Windows' wallpaper.

Apart from the picturesque views, I find that the American educational system is quite different from the Chinese system. With my major in journalism, I am deeply impressed by what I have experienced. One example can illustrate what I want to imply. In China, in my Journalist Writing class, the teacher would dwell on theories, followed by some discussions. By the end of the term, every student is expected to hand in a news release using what has been taught in class. However, when I took the same class in Plattsburgh, I found the teaching approaches totally different. We bought a course book: AP (i. e. Associated Press), but the teacher would never talk about anything from the book; instead, we used it as reference. I still remember my first class when we were asked to practice preparing deadline news and I was shocked. The teacher gave us a topic: suppose a fire broke out in the house of the university president the night before. We were supposed to interview the teacher who would play different roles and provide us various sorts of information, by asking him all kinds of questions. When he announced "Begin!" I could only hear rapid typing on the keyboards and shortly afterwards a series of questions, leaving me no opportunity to raise questions. I was very slow in typing. Then, I could only ask the teacher questions when others had actually started their writing! Besides, we played games in class, which, according to the teacher, is equivalent to a test of what we should learn in the textbooks. That means we need to have a good command of the knowledge in the textbook even though the teacher does not cover it in class. We also did a project named "People on the Street Story." Usually the teacher would give a topic such as "What do you think of President Obama's handling the economy?" We would decide on the interviewees accordingly, obtaining data, taking notes, and writing a news release. On the whole, we have benefited a lot from this course and learned that the American education focuses more on the participation of the students rather than theoretical knowledge only. The teacher also can give individual attention to each student, as the size of class is small, with only twenty students.

Apart from learning, I have also made many friends—teachers, classmates or cafeteria staff. I have also made some intimate friends, whom I can share

At Britt's dorm, May 2009

feelings and emotions with. My first good friend is a girl from Canada, very pretty, and a hockey-player, through whom I got to know several hockey-playing girls. We often visited each other in the dormitory, exchanging information and understanding. Venassa, a good friend I made when I was auditing Editing, helped me a lot with my study. From her I learned some customs of the American people, and it was her that I always turned to for help whenever I met with frustration. Alex, a classmate in Spanish class, is also my good friend. He is the only DJ in the university and a man with many ideas. Thanks to him, my life in the USA became colorful and meaningful. Whenever there was an activity coming up, he would tell me and thus I went to many live concerts, BBQs and spring carnival, etc. Dan, a good friend I met in Mass Media class, taught me a lot: how to use software such as Photoshop,

May 2009, with Lewis in front of the library

Moviemaker, and photography. Lewis, another good friend, always gave me unfailing help. I still remember my first Spanish class. As Americans have different approaches to language teaching, I felt it difficult to learn this language and I always turned to him for help. He explained everything to me carefully and patiently, and always offered me timely help. There are many other friends and teachers who have made my life interesting.

One year's overseas study is too short for me—but it is long enough to change my life. I was told that I look different from before. I have a better awareness of how I can manage my future life.

With First Lady of New York State, April 2009. The First Lady of New York State invited us to Albany to plant trees for memory.

He Juan, from Chongzhou City, Sichuan Province.

I study Journalism at Chengdu University of Technology. In America, I studied at SUNY – Plattsburgh. I'm extroverted and adventurous, and I like to make friends and also have a lot of friends around. Before I went to the US for studying, I have a lot of friends at home; and now, I have more friends abroad. What's more, I'm diligent in my study and works. I like challenges, it makes me feel exited and makes me grow up faster. I spread my wings and learn how to fly in my life, I'll do whatever it takes till I touch the sky.

A Visit to the USA

By Zhang Weiwei
Southwest University of Science and Technology

USA, a familiar yet strange country, has attracted so many people with its open and free cultural background, though it definitely cannot compare with our mysterious history of 5,000 years. It draws the world around it with its strong financial foundation. My early idea of the USA was based on guesswork but it was quite illusory and visionary, not yet proved with any experience and evidence until my trip to the USA during which I experienced the American culture, its systems and ways of life, which has benefited me a lot in my understanding of this country.

Many differences exist between China and the States, so novelty and curiosity kept us too busy to be homesick. I was intoxicated by the fantastic night views of the Fifth Avenue and the peacefulness and quietness of Plattsburgh. The bustling and prosperous metropolitan city life has always attracted many young people, so New York, a world financial center, has considerably fascinated me, a student in Economics.

After a few visits to New York, I was quite struck by the economic development of this metropolitan city with its prosperous urban views and crowds of people, but also excited by some invisible aspects. People have been too preoccupied with their pursuit for money and commodities to care about culture. During the winter break, I stayed in New York for one week, where a few things have considerably changed me, one of which is the biggest museum in Manhattan—a place to accumulate knowledge, to spread cultures, and to sublime one's spirit. I still feel excited at the thought about this museum. Visiting this museum is more intoxicating than overlooking the whole city from the Empire State

Building or searching for freedom at the foot of the Statue of Liberty. On the day trip to the museum, it was drizzling and the cold wind was blowing so hard that one would prefer to stay indoors. But great curiosity drove me on the way to exploration. I had planned to visit the museum in the morning and the botanical garden in the afternoon. After entering the museum, I knew that I would stay there the whole day. The 20-dollar admission fee can open a magic window for many people. The first sight that caught my eyes was the fanciful facilities, surrounded by children accompanied by their parents, or groups of students. I couldn't help going over trying to find out, and I found that the first floor was the introduction center to astronomy and the devices I had seen are used to introduce mysteries of the universe ranging from the Big Bang to the first human landing on the moon, in fact all the detailed information about the universe, and the next room is designated to exhibit space exploration. All these had inspired me. By chance, I left the first floor

On April 24, 2009, planting trees for friendship between China and America, with First Lady of New York State at New York State Goverener's Mansion

and went into another area and found on display varieties of rocks and fossils, indicating climatic changes and biological environment of living organisms. I was stunned to find how short life can be! I hardly had time to fully enjoy the variety of rare fossils; I walked to the center of the museum where you can find floras and fauna of all species, vegetation and trees either extinct or existing. I felt delighted but sorry when I saw children crouching in front of the exhibits busy taking notes; satisfied to see that these kids now have such a good opportunity to understand all creatures in the world, but sorry when thinking of the children in my hometown who do not have such condition and privilege. How I wished to be able to remember what I had seen here and share it with the kids in my hometown. In the short space of a few hours I seemed to have visited the whole universe. Though I stayed here the whole day, I still had many regrets: only if I could study every part and study everything in detail! But these regrets set in motion one of my ambitions: I will establish a world-class museum so as to give the kids in my hometown the same opportunity to learn and to broaden their vision. With this aim in mind, I found my life and studying so meaningful.

My visit to the museum gave me an opportunity to experience the respect that the Americans have for culture, their maturity and advancement in science and technology, while my life in Plattsburgh let me experience the American customs and lives.

On August 31, 2008, BBQ outside my dormitory

Plattsburgh, a small town, is located in the north of New York, about six or seven hours' drive from New York. Due to its small size, we could well feel the simplicity of the local inhabitants. Great difference exists between American cities and suburbs where you can feel the picturesque views and scenery, quiet, fresh air and blue sky. The clouds in the sky look very much like some art work. Here the kids are very active and carefree. At the university, you may find students from all over the world with diversified life styles and habits. I have learned a lot about the cultures and habits in many countries, of which the American way of life is most relaxing. In this way of life Americans can always deal with their study or life in a leisurely pace and they always have rich and exciting extracurricular activities. For example, we would often host BBQs, partly for communication and partly for fun. Sometimes the university would hire some amusement facilities like those in the amusement park to enrich students' extracurricular life. I was always overwhelmed at the nature of playfulness of American children. One game is Hit and Fall, i. e., one child sits on a wooden plank which is attached to a switch. Under the plank is a big bucket full of water. Other kids will use balls to hit the switch. Once the switch is hit, the kid sitting on the plank will fall into the water underneath. I remember thinking it must be impossible for anyone to volunteer to be the victim and there must be some procedures to

May 23, 2009, farewell party in the Consulate-General of the P. R. C. in New York. People (from left to right): The wife of Consul General Peng Keyu, me, Consul General Peng Keyu and Edward Cox, the son-in-law of the former American President Nixon.

decide who will be the one to sit on the plank. After some observation, I found some kids would be happy to sit on the plank and fall into the water without unhappiness or complaint, instead they were as happy as those throwing balls even when they were soaking wet. I was quite impressed at the loveliness of the American kids. Whatever they do, they will do that whole-heartedly, enjoying their participation. In fact they have some long-term life plans while they still feel free to enjoy every moment of their lives.

During the course of the year in the States, I experienced something unique: the smiles and hugs of the university cafeteria women staff, kind help of the ISS workers, instructions of the tutors and professors, the graciousness and entertainment of the American Chinese in Chinatown, tree planting for friendship between China and America at New York State Governor's Mansion and the farewell party in the Consulate-General—all these have left me deep and vivid impressions. I am sure how much theoretical knowledge I have learned but the feelings and understandings in the year have left a mark on me, which will help me cope with life more sensibly and competently.

Actualization of dreams = Willpower + Boldness + Capability

Zhang Weiwei, from Dujiangyan City, Sichuan Province.

I study Economics at Southwest University of Science and Technology. In America, I studied at SUNY – Plattsburgh. My dream is to build a world-class museum in China and have my own global chain of flower garden.

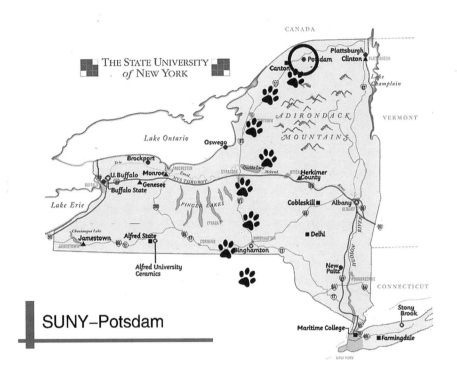

CANADA

Plattsburgh
Clinton

Potsdam

Canton

Lake Champlain

VERMONT

Lake Ontario

Oswego

A D I R O N D A C K

M O U N T A I N S

Brockport

U. Buffalo   Monroe
BUFFALO
Buffalo State

Lake Erie

ROCHESTER   SYRACUSE   *Oneida Lake*   Mohawk   Utica   Herkimer County

NYS THRUWAY

Genesee

FINGER LAKES

ITHACA

Cobleskill   Albany
ALBANY

Chautauqua Lake

Jamestown
JAMESTOWN

Alfred State

CORNING   BINGHAMTON

Binghamton

Delhi

Alfred University
Ceramics

New
Paltz

POUGHKEEPSIE

CONNECTICUT

Stony
Brook

Maritime College

Farmingdale

NEW YORK

SUNY–Potsdam

The Unforgettable Year

By *Wang Yingxue*
Chengdu University of Technology

In July 2008, luck befell me with the care and love from all over the world: after numerous interviews, I was given a valuable opportunity to study in the United States. After a short but miraculous period of preparation, together with the other 149 students from the severely hit areas in the devastating Wenchuan Earthquake, we gratefully set off on a journey to the United States.

Our journey drew extensive attention from the government and the society: from the intensive training in Sichuan University, and the visit of the Minister of Education, to the gracious greetings at JFK International Airport and the hospitality from the staff in the Consulate-General of the P. R. C. in New York and the generous donations from the American Chinese in the Chinatown. All of us received careful care and deep concern all the way. Standing in the bustling city of New York, we were deeply attracted by its charm. We were struck by this prosperous city, with its solemn Statue of Liberty, the busy Times Square, the skyscraping building complexes of the World Trade Center and the luxurious and charming Fifth Avenue.

The 150 students were assigned to twenty-two universities of SUNY, and I was in Potsdam, which is the northernmost campus of SUNY, with less than one hour's drive from Canada. As a young person who lives in the magnificent Land of Abundance with its mild climate, I was intoxicated by the ice and snow in this northern region.

But of course there would be cultural clashes when we came to a new area. And we were quite curious about many people and events. The local inhabitants in the town greeted and smiled to us. At the beginning we were afraid and surprised, but later on we came to realize that friendship is the most spectacular treasure in this quiet town. Americans are very open, free in speech and casual in dressing. They often have parties, which were too noisy for us to fall asleep, which really annoyed me. We also found something shocking. For example, Americans don't care about current affairs and they even don't know who is the Canadian president, let alone the happenings in China. They often asked us some simple questions such as "Have you got Wal-Mart in China?" "Have you got any textbooks?" All these differences kept me puzzled and frustrated. But with the passage of time, I got accustomed to these differences and came to enjoy the unique culture of this country.

My first canoeing experience in Potsdam Park

Our trip to the USA has attracted the attention of many local communities. When they learned that we came from the Sichuan earthquake-hit area, they prayed for us and the people in our hometown, which considerably impressed us. My American friends and host family often invited us to dinners and parties. It was because of these friends that I tasted American family-made meals and experienced exciting canoeing trips.

In this year, I made many friends from all over the world: USA, Switzerland, Germany, Japan, and Korea. We opened ourselves to different cultures. The most memorable in this year is the friendship I had with so many wonderful friends. This cross-border friendship shone throughout this year and I believe it will continue eternally.

It is difficult to study abroad, but I have benefited greatly from the study in the two semesters: knowledge from books, combination of theory and practice, practical and problem-solving skills and creative thinking. In the first semester, due to my poor English, I chose some easy courses, but still felt heavy stress as we must make good use of our time to study more to make up for the deficiency of knowledge. As writing and intensive reading are the essential skills in many courses, every day I had to spend about eight hours working in the library doing homework, reviewing and previewing. When exams were coming up, I had to stay up late at night reviewing courses, as we Chinese won't easily give up. It was this never-yielding spirit that inspired us to study hard and become the top students in the class. All the 150 students got good GPA. Hard as it was, I found the experience and great efforts very rewarding and valuable when we were awarded the certificate of SUNY.

The United States is a beautiful country, especially in autumn and winter in the north. Stepping on the golden leaves, you can hear the creaking sounds on the ground. Lying on the thick leaves, you will be enveloped in the golden color. Entering the forest, you will see the golden, green and red leaves leaving mottled shadows in the sunshine.

The winter in the north came all of a sudden. On Nov. 30, 2008, I experienced the first snow in the States. I shouted and burst into the thick snow that had piled up in less than two hours, taking photos, fighting with snowballs. But this snow lasted till the end of next April. For half a year, we lived in a world of snow. In this winter, the university organized a trip to Montreal, the former French colony. I was deeply attracted by the European style. My friends Jessica and Ryan drove us to Ottawa, the capital city of Canada, and we were shocked by the majestic building complexes on Capitol Hill. I also traveled over ten cities by using the money I earned from my part-time job. All these added to the excitement of the year's study in the USA.

It seemed just like yesterday that we went to the States but today we have to say goodbye. On the day we left Potsdam, I did not cry. But I said to myself quietly: Goodbye, my love.

On the last night at the Consulate-General of the P. R. C. in New York, all the students and teachers cried and shed tears. All of us were

February 1, 2009, I had my birthday party in America. A lot of friends came to celebrate my birthday!

moved. One of the students said "This is the last night we are here in the States. Let us cry to our heart's content. "

Upon my return to China, I put down in my diary: I was surrounded by love, shedding tears of happiness. New York, I love you.

The youth is shining now, and I applaud for my youth.

Wang Yingxue, from Chongzhou City, Sichuan Province.

I am a student from Chengdu University of Technology, majoring in English. In America, I studied at SUNY − Potsdam. I am a hard-working girl who loves study and work, with positive attitudes. I am an out-going girl who loves dancing, and I made a lot of friends from around the world in the year 2008 to 2009. I learned valuable knowledge and earned recognition in the United States.

Gratitude and Responsibility

By Liu Yisheng
Leshan Normal University

When Sichuan, my hometown, was hit by the devastating earthquake, the Chinese Government and other provinces gave us great care and help. Premier Wen Jiabao went to the disaster area right after the earthquake and quickly mobilized from around the country more than ten million People's Liberation Army soldiers to participate in disaster relief; and governments at all levels kept putting the people's interests first; the slogan of "Save, save, and save" moved us all the time. With the correct leadership of the Communist Party and the Government, we overcame many difficulties and cured the sufferings brought by the natural disaster.

In July 2008, when we were recovering slowly from the the earthquake, exciting news came from the Ministry of Education that the State University of New York in the United States had offered 150 university students from the earthquake-stricken area the opportunity of one-year study. To make the study trip possible, the CSC would pay for air tickets while the relevant universities in China would help students get the application for passports and visas. This series of care had considerably moved us; thus before departure we were determined to study hard in the USA, to make considerable contribution to the society as well as the reconstruction of our hometowns and to achieve self-fulfillment.

As we arrived in JFK International Airport, the officials from the Consulate-General of the P. R. C. in New York went to the airport to meet us, which made us feel the warmth of our motherland in a foreign country. On the second day of our arrival in New York, we went to the Chinatown where we were given a grand welcome party by overseas

Chinese. We sampled abundant delicious Chinese food and received red envelopes representing the best wishes of the overseas Chinese. Later in the Consulate-General, Consul General Peng Keyu led all the staff in greeting us warmly, and made a passionate speech to motivate us. We were very excited and inspired, determined that we must work hard to study, making great efforts to contribute to the community in return for their help.

We met the teachers in charge from all the universities of SUNY in the Consulate-General, which was home to us when we were in the US. Here we felt the deep care and concern from Consul General and all the other working staff. After meeting with the teachers from SUNY, we left the Consulate-General of the P. R. C. in New York. We knew that we really left home and started our life and study in a foreign country.

In the first semester, I focused on the appreciation of and adjustment to the American society and culture. During Thanksgiving and Christmas, many locals invited us to their homes. I was enjoying this atmosphere of an American festival while introducing many traditional Chinese festivals such as Mid-Autumn and Spring Festival, etc. During the World Culture Week held in the town where our university is located, I attended the demonstration on behalf of the Chinese in the university. The game of using chopsticks to pick up table tennis balls was very popular among the local Americans. It gave them an opportunity to learn about chopsticks and table tennis in China. During the holidays, we also visited big cities in the USA, gaining a better understanding of the life and the cultures in this country. We also made some typical Sichuan food such as hotpot for our friends in order to give them some ideas about our catering culture while sampling our delicious food.

With my American friends

In the second semester, I got accustomed to all my surroundings. In April, I organized volunteer groups to donate food and clothing for poverty-stricken people in the north of New York. Such an activity was endorsed by many students from my university and they donated their clothing and the like. I took pleasure in helping other people and contributing to the society. This optimistic and be-kind-to-others attitude helped me make many intimate friends: an American elderly lady who gave me a bowl of strawberries when she happened to know I liked strawberries very much, a special friend who talked with me for a long time, and those who invited me to parties every week. I gained pleasure while I was creating pleasure for others. Before going back to China, we were invited by the First Lady of New York State to plant a tree representing Sino-American friendship at New York State Governor's Mansion. I hope that our friendship will grow like this tree.

I will always remember the tears shed by my friends at our departure, the scenes when all the canteen staff came out to say goodbye, the tears we shed when saying goodbye to each other at the station. I will take advantage of all the positive changes in myself and achieve self-fulfillment.

Upon my return to China, we could always feel the concern coming to us from the society and community. When setting foot on my motherland, we felt like children coming back to their mothers' arms. We also pledge to make use of what we have learned to contribute to the construction of our motherland and to be a person with a sense of gratitude and a sense of responsibility.

Liu Yisheng, from Deyang City, Sichuan Province.

I study at Leshan Normal University. During my nine months in the US, I studied at SUNY – Potsdam.

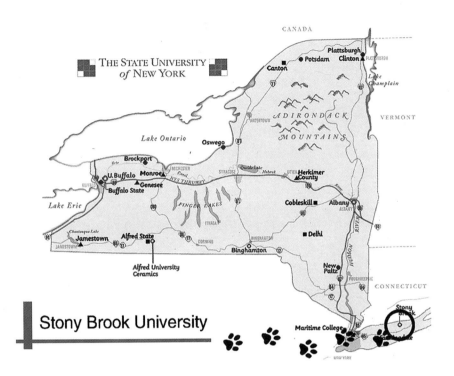

THE STATE UNIVERSITY of NEW YORK

Stony Brook University

A Travel Experience in America

By Zhang Liang
Sichuan University

In the United States I missed my hometown so much, and the feeling got stronger as I was approaching home. At last, I came back to my motherland.

Walking on the uneven pavement of Linyin Street, walking among bustling people on the campus of Sichuan University, I strongly felt, for the first time so strongly, the existence of my hometown and my motherland. The nine-month study in the United States, though short, left me so many recollections and contemplations. I gained a lot and I grew more mature.

Over a year ago, on my summer vacation, I got an unexpected notice about the CSC-SUNY 150 Program sponsored by the China Scholarship Council and collaborated by the State University of New York. This program aims to enable the Chinese students from the earthquake-stricken area to study in the United States. After application and two rounds of interviews within one week, I was lucky to become one of the 150 Chinese students. Marveling at the efficiency of the program, I sincerely thanked the teachers and employees who made my dream of travelling to the United States come true and really appreciated the American friends who provided me with such a good opportunity. I happily prepared for my journey to the United States, like the other twenty-five Sichuan University students with different experiences and majors, looking forward to the nine-month life abroad.

On August 13, all of us 150 students from Sichuan gathered at Sichuan University. I eventually saw the other students from the other universities, five of whom would go with me to the State University of New York at Stony Brook to spend nine months.

On August 15, we left for our destination—the United States.

After a short stay in New York City, on August 17, I, together with the other five students, went to Stony Brook University in the north of the Long Island of New York State. It was the first time for us to meet the counselor in charge of international students. It was the first time for us to come to a campus in the depth of the vast green broad-leaved forest on the Long Island. It was the first time for us to communicate with our tutor in somewhat broken English. A new university, a new country and a new culture, all these gave us newcomers fresh feelings, which motivated us to achieve something on this very land.

Then, the semester began. We started to attend classes; meanwhile, many expected and unexpected problems occurred constantly.

The first problem I met was a hard nut to crack. As a student of medical science, I did not know how to arrange my one-year courses. China's medical education system differs greatly from the American one in that the former begins its medical education at the undergraduate level while the latter at the postgraduate

My performance in the Chinese Embassy, Washington D. C. on January 8, 2009

level. Dr. Steven London, Deputy Dean of the School of Dental Medicine at Stony Brook University, in charge of teaching affairs, talked with me many times so as to set up my one-year curriculum, and also asked the subject teachers to offer me help. At last, Dr. London said to me humorously, "I know it is the first time for you to study overseas, and it is also the first time for me to deal with your case. Let's make joint efforts to get things done. " He took out a thick pile of documents and put them in front of me, saying: "All these are the materials I have used for setting up your curriculum." As the Deputy Dean in the well-known School of Dental Medicine, Dr. London settles down the problem for an ordinary student. His dedication is something I admire and the first lesson I learned after I had come to the United States.

After that, I began my busy and interesting campus life with my classmates.

Homecoming Day at Stony Brook University, on October 19, 2008

This semester, I observed the grand occasion of Homecoming Day, experienced the crazy shopping on Black Friday before Thanksgiving, visited the National Museum of Natural History where the movie *Night at the Museum* was filmed, and learned the customs of Christmas in conventional western families.... One semester passed by without knowing! Upon our arrival, the Long Island was covered with green trees, but now white snow could be seen here and there. We had never seen such a heavy snow in Sichuan, so we were very excited. Then we put on big boots, staggering on the snowfield, but we got used to them soon.

The environment was not new to us any longer, and we could even direct ways for newcomers. We already had a good mastery of English. Looking back, I suddenly found half of the time for my overseas study passed by, but I learned a lot.

On the winter vacation, I went from New York City to Washington D. C.

Goodbye, my friends. Suffolk County, New York on May 21, 2009

The winter vacation was the most wonderful one in my student life. In the IZOD Center of NBA, New Jersey, I watched the NBA basketball match between Nets and Rockets, or more well-known as the match between Yi Jianlian and Yao Ming, the two Chinese players. In New York City, I visited the Fifth Avenue, the tall Christmas tree in the Rockefeller Center and the skating rink below the tree. The Wall Street seemed to tell me its story of a once-prosperous Financial Empire. The erect one-century-old Empire State Building silently showed me the vicissitudes and glory of the city and the country in the past one hundred years. The Washington Monument, the tallest architecture in Washington D. C., witnessed how the most powerful country on this planet came into being by fighting against the British colonies in the Independence War centuries ago. I am lucky that I saw with my own eyes many places that I could only have seen in movies or on TV.

While I was studying and traveling in the United States, I never forgot my hometown which suffered from the devastating earthquake in 2008. Our folks are waiting for us to come back to participate in the reconstruction. As a student from the earthquake-stricken area, I must take the very responsibility for making contributions to my hometown after coming back from my study in the United States. It was not long for me to pursue my knowledge overseas, but my experiences there will, I believe, be beneficial to me all my life.

Where there is a will, there is a way.

Zhang Liang, from Deyang City, Sichuan Province.

I study Dental Medicine at China West College of Stomatology, Sichuan University. I spent nine months in the US, where I went to School of Dental Medicine, Stony Brook University.

My Study in the USA

By Liu Shan
Leshan Normal University

Nine months is long but still very short in one's lifetime; it is short but still long as it covers three quarters of a year. In my first few days in the USA, I just listened to other people and observed what others were doing, but could not find an opportunity to open my mouth. I was in a panic then, not knowing how I could survive the coming nine months in this strange land.

Fortunately, the university had arranged for us a psychologist who asked us to meet him once a week. Though at each meeting we just talked about our daily life briefly, it was important that he drew on his experience and told us some cultural differences between China and the US so as to help us fit in our environment as quickly as possible. Meanwhile, many Stony Brook University staff gave us much help, showing us around the campus, helping us to adjust to the university and our new life, and inviting us to their homes. The teachers even bought some Chinese food, the best they could find in the local area to comfort us nostalgic students.

There, I experienced choosing courses on my own for the first time in my life. I found it very frustrating to choose courses as I did not get used to the new environment and I had to consider whether I could understand the courses before choosing them. Besides, as many courses require prerequisite courses, many of us could not choose our specialist courses as we hadn't taken any prerequisite ones. Luckily, since there was so much for me to learn in my specialty, there was not too much trouble for me to choose my courses. What impressed me deeply is Design of

With Counselor Education Cen Jianjun

Computer Game. I used to think that computer games were just about compiling code; for RPG, you simply needed to add a synopsis of the story. After taking this course, I learned that every game has feedback, both positive and negative. Only when they are closely interlinked can the game be a meaningful and feasible one. Another example is Game Theory. In class, the teacher not only gave us the necessary game theories, but also collected for us the most popular game designing concepts such as Spore, its design concepts, content, and the process of actualization. All these made me aware of my limitations in the understanding of game design. This course also requires the students to form teams in their game design, write independently the design concept, the steps of design, diagrams of design, and its draft, and finally present it to other teams. With the combination of theory and practice, every student could understand the process of game design. What is also worth mentioning is the Advanced Programming with

With Nixon's daughter

UNIX & C. This course made me aware how limited my expertise was in my major and gave me lots of inspiration. I realized the significance of code portability and the reason for the various versions of operating systems. In short, the nine months in Stony Brook University enabled me to understand more deeply the combination of theory and practice. In fact, it is easy to forget the theories you have read. Only when you have applied it to practice can you understand its underlying concepts. Attitude can determine the outcome, so you can make achievements only when you actually engage in the application of the theory.

Another aspect is the improvement of my competence in work. Luckily, I got an opportunity to work in the Foreign Affairs Office where I only did such simple work as sorting out materials and publicizing activities of foreign affairs. As the saying goes, effort brings success. All the trivial work contributes to great achievement, and so was the case with my work in the office. I learned how to deal with strangers, how to carry out publicity in foreign affairs and how to sort out documents and files in the office. In addition, I also participated in the Residence Security Program in which students had to take sole responsibility for its management and arrangement to ensure the safety of resident students. In the program, I worked with other students to solve problems and exchange experiences. From them, I have benefited a lot, and I formed my own viewpoints about many issues, learned about many different cultures and customs in many countries, broadened my horizon and improved my communicative skills.

With my conversation teachers

I must also mention the Conversation Club, which aims at improving our oral English and communicative skills. Every week, teachers would arrange the topics for each conversation, some about social problems, some about arguments about heated issues and some about life planning. With all the diversity of conversation topics, I

benefited significantly in the course of conversations and acquired brief but idiomatic expressions, new vocabulary and phrases, etc.

On the whole, the nine months in Stony Brook University gave me a completely new but rewarding life, with constant improvement and new ideas replacing old ones. In the course of such acquisition and alternation of new and old, I have learned how to sensibly analyze and solve problems. I hope to keep this attitude and capacity of accepting new ideas, to consolidate this experience and make good use of it so as to build a better future for myself.

Liu Shan, from Jiangyou City, Sichuan Province.

I study at Department of Computer Science and Information Technology in Leshan Normal University. During my nine months in the US, I studied at Stony Brook University.

On the Year of Study in US

By Zhang Rui

Chengdu University of Information Technology

On May 12, 2008, unexpected massive earthquake attacked Sichuan, resulting in the fact that many people lost their family members and left their homes. After the disaster, with the concern of the CPC Central Committee and the State Council as well as the assistance of those loving people from all walks of life, CSC-SUNY 150 Program came into being to provide 150 university students from the earthquake-stricken area with an opportunity to study at SUNY for one year.

I was lucky enough to be one of the 150 students in this program to study Applied Math and Statistics at State University of New York, Stony Brook University.

With its beautiful environment and strong faculty, Stony Brook University enabled me to achieve a lot in this year.

Study

When the new semester began, I learned that there was a department in the university that would help students to choose courses and each student could meet his advisor. In American universities, students don't have to decide on their majors when they enter the university. Actually many students choose their majors after one or two years. When choosing your major, it is necessary to consult your advisor or the professors in that major. You can tell the advisor your interest and he will give you some advice regarding the choice of majors (of course this is just a suggestion, not obligatory). After you have chosen the courses, you have two weeks

for sit-in to observe(sit-in periods vary from university to university); in this way you can decide whether the course is suitable for you. Some demanding courses require prerequisite courses and you have to pass them before choosing more difficult ones.

In American universities, tests are quite common, with three or four in each semester, in addition to quizzes and homework. As these account for a large proportion of the final grade. Everyone has to make greater efforts to prepare for these tests. Otherwise even with a full mark for the final he may fail the course if he shows poor performance in his tests.

You are bound to meet with some difficulties in study. In the university, you can go to the professor for help, who is always available in the office in his office hours. Out of the office hours, there are also teaching assistants for some difficult courses. They are usually post-graduates in their respective majors who can usually give us much help in problem solving. Apart from these face-to-face meetings, you can also contact the professors or teaching assistants via email, which is also an effective way to get help.

Besides, whatever your major is, you have to take many optional courses, which cover a wide range. For example, a math student has to take some optional courses in other fields in addition to his own obligatory major. These optional courses may involve Economics, Commerce, Environment, Geography, Music and Art and other social courses. These courses can enrich the knowledge of the students, which may be beneficial to their majors and contribute to their accumulation of social knowledge. During this period, some students can even find the courses they really like and then transfer to their relative courses. So this teaching approach is quite dynamic, considerably facilitating their choice of courses.

Daily life

At Stony Brook University, I had many memorable moments, which are most interesting.

Roth Pond Regatta is an annual grand event in this university. Every spring, when the weather is clear and sunny, the university will host boat races in Roth Pond. But this race is different from other boat races as the boats are all made by environmentally friendly materials to protect the environment, so there are varieties of boats such as Caribbean pirate, Chinese dragon, car model—the game is to compete for reaching the finishing line.

Roth Pond Regatta, a traditional event in Stony Brook University

Strawberry Festival is another important annual event at Stony Brook University, which is very popular with students. At every strawberry festival, the university will make all kinds of food out of strawberry: strawberry ice cream, barbecue with strawberry jam, strawberry juice, and strawberry chocolate. You only need one ticket to sample all kinds of strawberry food. Isn't it a pleasure to be in nature tasting delicious food in the bright sunshine?

Orientation Week for New Students. In the spring semester, I participated as a volunteer in the orientation of international students. In

this Orientation Week, we needed to meet new students and arranged a lot of activities to help new students to adapt themselves to new life on campus: copying materials for them, arranging meetings, answering all sorts of questions from the new students and taking them on a campus tour. I benefited considerably from this orientation week. Consequently, I have improved my English level, developed my organizing skills and made many friends from different parts of the world: France, China, South Korea, Japan and India. Like us, they were full of curiosity and puzzles when they just arrived. We made efforts to get to know their puzzles so as to help them.

In retrospect, I found the year in the US very rewarding. I can clearly see my achievements not only in the improvement of my English but also in the broadening of my horizon. This year's experience has given me more confidence. I will ponder more sensibly about my future and be more resolute to do what I intended to do. As a student from Wenchuan earthquake-hit area, I greatly cherish the one-year study in the USA. With the best wishes and expectations of those people in my hometown, we studied very hard in different universities at SUNY, made great achievements and experienced the multicultural life. This year has given me valuable experience from the cultural diversity. Upon my return to China, I will bring back my experience to my hometown to contribute to its reconstruction. CSC-SUNY 150 Program is an indicator of the Sino-American friendship. As one of the participants, I will act as an envoy and spare no efforts to promote the friendship between the two countries. Only when I was outside China did I feel the strength my country has empowered me and understand the responsibility I must take. I know better that what I do and say must be for the benefit of my country and people. I could not understand them until now that my great motherland has given me limitless strength and support, with which I will strive to achieve self-fulfillment and my aim. Meanwhile, I will pass on the love and care I received to benefit others.

I will cherish everything around me, and I will think about my future more carefully.

Zhang Rui, from Chongzhou City, Sichuan Province.

I study Statistics at Chengdu University of Information Technology. It is my great honor to have this opportunity to be taken part in CSC-SUNY 150 Program, to be admitted in Stony Brook University, and go on my own major—Applied Math and Statistics. In my spare time, I pay some attention to the current news about China or the rest of the world. Because of this, I spent lots of time studying English in order to get informed about different views. Besides, travelling is also my favorite, I like to experience various life styles and cultures. Moreover, I enjoy music, modern or classic, so in Stony Brook University I cherished every chance to listen to the concerts. In addition, I chose a special course in Stony Brook University named "First Aid," which can help others in emergency. Through my effort, I got the certificate from American Red Cross.

Nine Months, a New Start

By Yang Xi

Chengdu University of Information Technology

At 2: 28 p. m. on May 12, 2008, an unexpected disaster struck Sichuan, my hometown, where numerous people were killed and buildings were devastated. We were in despair and helplessness when help was pouring in from all over the country: goods and volunteer for disaster relief—we deeply felt the concern and care of the people in my homeland. Meanwhile, foreign countries also offered their help in forms of materials

and money. State University of New York offered 150 university students from the earthquake-hit area a full scholarship to study there for one academic year. After an intense period of application, interview and retest, I was fortunate enough to be one of the 150 students. On Aug. 15, 2009, we took a flight to the US.

This picture was taken at Stony Brook University's school gate when I first arrived there in September 2008. New people, new environment, everything is new to me...

Upon my arrival in the USA, I was attracted by the new: blue sky, the skyscraping Empire State Building and the bustling Fifth Avenue. Everyday I could see people of different races, and as a newcomer I felt a sense of novelty and curiosity and a bit fear when meeting with these people. But soon I found my fear unnecessary and I was amazed by their enthusiasm. They took great interest in games we found trivial or took no notice of. At first I thought of them as childish but soon discovered that it was not their childish play but rather our lack of enthusiasm in ourselves.

Perhaps because of our majors, I was assigned with other students to Stony Brook University, one of the four biggest universities of SUNY, which is located in the east of New York City and the northern bank of the Long Island. Nobel Laureate Professor Yang Zhenning had taught thirty years at this university. There are many students from Asia, accounting for over a half of the total number of international students. Whenever you walk on campus, you can meet groups of Chinese students.

An English learning conversation group in Stony Brook University. The members were from all walks of life. My knowledge of the United States enriched a lot from this conversation group.

At first, the greatest challenge for me was attending classes in my major as I didn't understand the teachers. I had to work much longer than others when I went back to my dorm. Gradually, with the increasingly large command of vocabulary, I understood more in class. The teachers would come up with many novel ideas to attract students to participate in class activities, rather than just talk by themselves.

What impressed me most in the nine months' life in the US is the independence of American students. They will not take for granted what we consider natural. Once I was talking to a friend called Lisa. She said that she would visit China after graduation, so she was working hard to earn enough money for her travel. I was surprised and said that she could go to her parents for help. She looked at me in surprise and said: "Why should they pay for me? I can make money by myself. " Seeing that I was puzzled, she added: "I know what you mean, but I don't want to do that and rely too much on them since I can make money by myself and pay for what I like. I feel good in this way. " For those of us born in the 1980s and 1990s, it is quite natural for us to go to the parents for help when we need money, but they regard it important to be independent ever since they enter university and pay for daily lives and tuition fee on their own. So many students take up part-time work, trying hard to find a sort of part-time job on which they can both earn money and improve their leadership. Many students also do some voluntary work, laying as much emphasis on experience and skills as kids in other countries. In fact this is part of the American culture: developing independence in children. So many students have their own specific plan or clear idea about their future when entering university in terms of their major, whether to study for a master's degree, where to work for a short time and even when and which

country to visit. This habit of planning ahead is something I really need to learn as I used to think that there was no need to make a plan and I only needed to take up whatever came to me. But now when I am back in China I feel that the most urgent thing is to make a comprehensive life plan for myself. One of

A particular and colourful dormitory in MIT

my classmates told me one day: "You may change your life plan someday, however it's important to know what matters most to you. "

My trip to the US has not only enriched my knowledge in my major but also broadened my horizons. During the winter break, during the Leadership Training Program, I finally saw the White House—the symbol of the American government. The streets of New York are bright and clean and those of Washington D. C. are full of castles with all pedestrians in black windbreakers and briefcases. Washington presents us with its long history and cultural heritage whereas Boston gives us a feeling of relaxation. And the world famous Harvard University and Massachusetts Institute of Technology add much charm to this city. Wandering on the campuses, I felt very calm and peaceful. Instead of just paying a visit, I felt that I was feeling these prestigious institutions of higher education with my heart....

During my one-year study in US, all kinds of people have given us help: the American professors are quite responsible and patient, which was very helpful to us who did not know much about the American education system; the teachers and leaders in China gave us great help in interviews and visa application until the day before we set off to the United States the teachers in the International Exchange Office were still carefully sorting out all matters regarding our trip. We kept close contact with all when we were in the US. Last year in November, Premier Wen Jiabao and Vice Chairman of the Standing Committee of the National People's Congress, Chen Zhili met some of us from the nearby universities at the Consulate-General when they went to New York for a conference, caring about our life and study and giving us the commemorative stamps for Olympic Games. In April of this year, State Councilor Liu Yandong came to visit us with Zhou Dingwen, the president of Chengdu University of Information Technology when she came for the opening ceremony of the Confucius Institute at Stony Brook University. We are the lucky group out of an inevitable unfortunate natural disaster, and the concern and care of these people can help us stand up quickly.

In retrospect, CSC-SUNY 150 Program is a miracle. The smiling faces of the 150 students have consolidated the bridge between China and the US, and there have been a lot of changes in our lives and values. We have learned about cherishing, gratitude and enthusiastic participation in collective work. My life has changed! We'd like to extend sincere thanks to those who have given us help. We are fortunate to be alive and can live a happy and pleasant life.

I have always believed that natural disaster led to a bad end but also a new start.

I'll use my gratitude heart to cherish and pass the love.

Yang Xi, from Ya'an City, Sichuan Province.

I have been studying at Chengdu University of Information Technology from 2006, majoring in Electronic Engineering. In America, I studied Electronic Engineering at Stony Brook University. Last year, after the earthquake in Sichuan, I got a chance to study in the USA for one year. During this year I experienced a colourful culture and learned how to deal with people from different backgrounds. I got more chances to think about myself and my future.

"China 150" Smiles Will Go On

University at Albany – SUNY

Forget about the political and cultural prejudices, and communicate with others as an individual, then we will find that we have the same human nature.

I'm Zhou Tao, from Pengzhou City, Sichuan Province. I study Chinese Language and Literature at Xihua University. In America, I studied Chinese Language and Literature at University at Albany – SUNY.

Study and live with ease, make my life full and realize the value of my life.

I'm Chen Hao, from Aba Tibetan and Qiang Autonomous Prefecture. I study Preventive Medicine at Sichuan University. During my nine months in the US, I attended University at Albany – SUNY.

Life is a process of fighting. Once you fall, stand up and keep fighting.

I'm Pi Meng, from Mianzhu City, Sichuan Province. I study at Chengdu University of Information Technology. My major is Atmospheric Science. In America, I went to University at Albany − SUNY. This experience is unforgettable to me. It was my first time to study abroad, which helped me get to know myself and what I should do in the future. I will study for one more year in Chengdu University of Information Technology before I graduate, and I will do my best to achieve my goal.

New York State College of Ceramics at Alfred University

No cross, no crown.

I'm Pan Huanhuan, from Jiangyou City, Sichuan Province. I study Metal Material at Southwest Petroleum University. From 2008 to 2009, I studied at New York State College of Ceramics at Alfred University.

Cherish · everything you have whenever or wherever you are.

I'm Chen Bing, from Mianyang City, Sichuan Province. I study Materials Science and Engineering at Southwest University of Science and Technology. In America, I studied Materials Engineering in New York State College of Ceramics at Alfred University.

It's hard but sweet to grow up.

I'm Zheng Yuanxin, from Mianyang City, Sichuan Province. I study Polymer Material and Engineering at Sichuan University. In America, I went to New York State College of Ceramics at Alfred University.

Alfred State College

For the whole year, only one sentence is the most useful one: Thank you all.

I'm Ma Xiaochuan, from Xiaojin County, Sichuan Province. I study at Sichuan University. In America, I studied at Alfred State College. In May, 2008, I participated in the Youth Volunteer Team of Manufacturing Science and Engineering College to help transport relief materials to the earthquake area at the Shuangliu International Airport. After that, I participated in the volunteer team in West China Hospital to help people find their family members, who were critically injured in the earthquake, from the hospital's name list.

SUNY – Binghamton University

I will create my future with a heart full of thanks.

I'm Ye Bo, from Pengzhou City, Sichuan Province. I studied Vehicle Engineering in School of Mechanical Engineering, Southwest Jiaotong University. From 2008 to 2009, I studied in SUNY – Binghamton University.

SUNY − The College at Brockport

Do not, for one repulse, forget the purpose
that you resolved to effort.

I'm He Ting, from Dujiangyan City, Sichuan Province. I study at College of Foreign Languages and Literature, Sichuan University. During my nine months in the US, I went to SUNY − The College at Brockport.

I'm Xu Lei, from Shifang City, Sichuan Province. I study English at Xihua University. I joined some clubs in my university. I had several essays published in the school newspaper and had three papers published. From 2008 to 2009, I studied at SUNY − The College at Brockport.

My name is Wen Yan, from Dujiangyan City, Sichuan Province. I study in the Department of Political Science and Law at Leshan Normal University. In America, I went to SUNY − The College at Brockport. I learned a lot of things during the past one year. I have not only improved my spoken English, but also learned how to take care of myself without my parents' help. The thing I cherish most is that I foster a really good relationship with my American friends and other international students.

SUNY − Buffalo State College

No matter where and when, just try it.

I'm Tan Ziwei, from Pengzhou City, Sichuan Province. I study at English Department of Sichuan University in China and studied at SUNY – Buffalo State College in America. In May, 2008, I helped deliver relief goods at the Shuangliu International Airport. In June, 2008, I visited and helped the victims of Wenchuan Earthquake in West China Hospital.

Life is full of changes, and we have to make good use of those opportunities.

I'm Sun Xuerui, from the hometown of the most famous poet—Li Bai—Jiangyou. I study English at Chengdu University of Information Technology. This year, I went to SUNY – Buffalo State College and studied English there. At Buffalo, I met the heavy snow I had never experienced in my life. I love Hockey and the adorable Bengal!

I'm Su Chang, from Mianzhu City, Sichuan Province. I study Finance at School of Economics in Sichuan University. I am a straightforward person. I like to help others in need. In addition, I always treat others with heart and soul. I love my major—Finance and I hope I can do something useful in my field as the reward to my beloved country—China.

There is no limit to you as there is no limit to your mind.

I'm Yin Xin, from Pengzhou City, Sichuan Province. I study Microelectronics at Southwest Jiaotong University. In America, I studied at SUNY – Buffalo State College. I am a cheerful, positive and optimistic girl. I love sports, I enjoy being with people and nature.

Life is full of mysteries, always hope for the best!

I'm Zhong Xue, from Deyang City, Sichuan Province. I study English Education at China West Normal University. From 2008 to 2009, I studied at SUNY – Buffalo State College. I feel so lucky to study abroad. I have got a lot from this study trip. I have learned a lot, and I have made many friends. This trip has broadened my horizons. I hope I can apply what I have learned to the reconstruction of my hometown.

Do a little everyday, get a lot someday.

I'm Deng Yanlin, from Jiangyou City, Sichuan Province. I study English at Southwest University of Science and Technology. In America, I studied at SUNY – Buffalo State College.

In our one-year life in America, we have harvested personal growth, as well as a grateful heart.

I'm Liang Ping, from Jiangyou City, Sichuan Province. I study English at Sichuan University. In America, I studied at SUNY – Buffalo State College. I am positive, optimistic and energetic; I can always find happiness in everyday life; I always care about others; I have good psychological quality, and I have a strong sense of independence.

I'm Deng Xia, from Mianzhu City, Sichuan Province. I study English at Leshan Normal University. In America, I went to SUNY – Buffalo State College.

I'm Shu Yuchan, from Deyang City, Sichuan Province. I study at Chengdu University of Technology. In America, I went to SUNY – Buffalo State College.

Do not put off till tomorrow what can be done today.

I'm Wang Longpan, from Wenchuan County, Sichuan Province. I study Law at Xihua University. From 2008 to 2009, I studied at SUNY – Buffalo State College.

New York State has given me a chance to know the outside world. I'll never let you down.

I'm Yuan Yue, from Wenchuan County, Sichuan Province. I study Law at China West Normal University. In America, I went to SUNY – Buffalo State College, majoring in Criminal Justice.

Farewell to kind of life and embark on a new one.

I'm Zheng Lin, from Shifang City, Sichuan Province. I study in English Department in Southwest Petroleum University. From 2008 to 2009, I studied in SUNY – Buffalo State College.

University at Buffalo – SUNY

It is love that has given me hope and dream. And I will convey and pass the love with a grateful heart, and to make everyone around me feel that love always stays with them.

I'm Yang Ran, from Deyang City, Sichuan Province. I study at Southwest Jiaotong University. During my nine months in the US, I went to University at Buffalo – SUNY.

No matter how many difficulties we will have to go through, I believe we will always find a way to cope with them. Because we are supported by the love of our family and other warm-hearted people.

I'm Ruan Tianyuan, from Guanghan City, Sichuan Province. I study in the School of Chemistry and Life Science, Sichuan University. In America, I studied at University at Buffalo – SUNY.

Everything is possible in this world.

I'm Dai Ting, from Pengzhou City, Sichuan Province. I study Industrial Engineering at Chengdu University of Technology. In America, I studied at University at Buffalo – SUNY.

SUNY – Canton

Wherever I go, whatever I do, you, China, is always in my heart.

I'm Ding Yong, from Deyang City, Sichuan Province. I'm a student of Southwest University of Science and Technology. In America, I studied Mechanical Engineering Technology at SUNY – Canton.

You would never know until you try.

I'm Zheng Miao, from Chongzhou City, Sichuan Province. I study Civil Engineering at Southwest Jiaotong University. During my nine months in the US. , I went to SUNY – Canton.

I'm Liu Xiaolin, from Pengzhou City, Sichuan Province. I study Petroleum Engineering at Southwest Petroleum University. From 2008 to 2009, I studied Engineering Science at SUNY – Canton.

Differences come from comparison, and lead to deeper thinking, which facilitates progress.

I'm Yang Ying, from Deyang City, Sichuan Province. I'm majored in Civil Engineering in Southwest University of Science and Technology. In America, I studied Civil Engineering Technician at SUNY – Canton. I'm outgoing and I like drawing, singing and playing volleyball.

SUNY has her memories of us, and we have our sweet memories of SUNY.

I'm Ju Dandan, from Shifang City, Sichuan Province. I study in School of English of International Trade in Southwestern University of Finance and Economics. From 2008 to 2009, I studied at SUNY – Canton.

SUNY – Clinton Community College

Love makes the world go around.

I'm Du Chang, from Deyang City, Sichuan Province. I study Psychology at Sichuan Normal University. In America, I studied Psychology at SUNY – Clinton Community College for one academic year.

I appreciate everything done by State University of New York, China Scholarship Council and people who helped us very much.

I'm Huang Lei, from Dujiangyan City, Sichuan Province. I am studying at Chengdu University of Information Technology. I major in Software Engineering. I studied at SUNY – Clinton Community College in the first semester in America, then transfered to Stony Brook University in the second semester.

I'm Xu Xin, from Dujiangyan City, Sichuan Province. I study Computer Science and Technology at University of Electronic Science and Technology of China. In America, I studied at SUNY − Clinton Community College.

A workman must first sharpen his tools if he is to do his work well.

I'm Yang Shixin, from Shifang City, Sichuan Province. I study at Sichuan University, majoring in International Politics. I went to SUNY − Clinton Community College during my first semester in America and transferred to Stony Brook University in the second semester.

I have learned the simplest lesson in my life abroad: draw a bottom line for happiness and learn to savour joy and bliss in the trivialest matters of ordinary life; cherish everything we have.

I'm Yuan Ye, from Dujiangyan City, Sichuan Province. I study Computer Science at China West Normal University. In America, I studied at SUNY − Clinton Community College. I am the protagonist of my own life. As a positive, confident girl, I like singing, design and communicating with others. I will try my best to bring people happiness all over the world. I do believe I will succeed in my life, because I must keep my own promise.

Love is everything.

I'm Liu Fengqian, from Mianzhu City, Sichuan Province. I study Administration Management at Chengdu University of Information Technology. After the earthquake, I got the chance to study at SUNY − Clinton Community College, which has influenced me so much. With the year passing by,

I learned how to live independently and how to forgive; Also, I learned to treat my life with appreciation and hope. I believe, love can touch everything.

The peace in heart is gold.

I'm Lu Yi, from Mianyang City, Sichuan Province. I am a student from Southwestern University of Finance and Economics, and my major is Accounting. In America, I studied at SUNY − Clinton Community College. In my spare time I like drawing, playing basketball (even though I am not good at it), taking pictures, and communicating with my friends. I am a patient girl and very eager to help others.

What we know about the world is less important than how we think about it.

I'm Xu Xingping, from Chongzhou City, Sichuan Province. I study English Education at China West Normal University. In America, I went to SUNY − Clinton Community College, majoring in English Language and Literature. I hope I can be a good translator in the future, building the bridge of communication between two cultures.

SUNY − Cobleskill

What a sweet life! Thanks for the people who walking with me on this beautiful journey.

I'm Pu Yibei, from Jiangyou City, Sichuan Province. I study Accounting at Southwestern University of Finance and Economics. In America, I studied Accounting at SUNY − Cobleskill. I love sweet food, spicy food, listening to others, traveling around the world, and living a simple and happy life.

The most precious thing given by the precious nine months is a thanksgiving heart.

I'm Zhao Ying, from Jiangyou City, Sichuan Province. I study Landscape at Sichuan Agricultural University. In America, I studied at SUNY − Cobleskill.

Thanks to the love and care around us, we grew up a lot and had new life experience in the past one year, which is also my unforgettable memory.

I'm Long Fei, from Guanghan City, Sichuan Province. I am a student of Southwestern University of Finance and Economics. From 2008 to 2009, I studied at SUNY − Cobleskill. This year in America introduced me to different people and different cultures. I have learned a lot, and have become more confident. The different way of thinking helped me to view things in a more comprehensive way. I also got many life experiences through travel. I always feel grateful because I know all of these wouldn't have happened without the help of so many people. Now it's time for us to spread the love to more people.

We left our home during the nine months, but we found another home across the ocean, with the same happiness and warmness.

I'm Lei Xiaoyu, from Beichuan, Sichuan, a place totally destroyed in the earthquake. I study at Southwestern University of Finance and Economics. In America, I studied at SUNY − Cobleskill. Quiet as I am, I'm fond of volleyball and badminton. I'm shy with strangers, but once I become familiar with you, it will be very hard to stop me from talking. I'm proud of my ability in logic

analysis. I love movies about the military and wars. Politics, military and economy are my favorite topics.

Chances are always for those who are well-prepared.

I'm Peng Lirong, from Mianyang City, Sichuan Province. I study Landscape at Sichuan Agricultural University. In America, I studied at SUNY – Cobleskill. My hobbies are drawing, singing and playing volleyball.

Remember and love those who have been loving you!

I'm Chen Chen, a Qiang Nationality from Beichuan County, Sichuan Province. I study Tourism Management at Sichuan University. From September 2008 to May 2009, I studied at SUNY – Cobleskill. I threw myself into volunteer activities immediately after the earthquake. During abroad, I was a member of the International Club in SUNY – Cobleskill.

I'm Xiao Junmei, from Mianyang City, Sichuan Province. I study Food Science and Engineering at Sichuan University. In America, I studied at SUNY – Cobleskill. In May, 2008, I volunteered to help the people in earthquake area in Dujiangyan. April 21, 2009, I helped the illiterates in a community of Schohaire County in America.

Be disciplined when you are poor; and be generous when you are rich.

I'm Lan Xue, from Mianyang City, Sichuan Province. I study Agriculture at Southwest University of Science and Technology. In America, I studied at SUNY - Cobleskill.

I'm Wen Huan, from Mianyang City, Sichuan Province. I study at Sichuan Normal University. In America, I studied at SUNY - Cobleskill.

During the short nine-months' overseas experience, I found myself growing up every day. I learnt how to think, how to appreciate, how to give and how to be independent. I was lucky to gain such great opportunity, and I will make it a new start.

I'm Deng Jing, from Mianyang City, Sichuan Province. I study Accounting at Southwestern University of Finance and Economics. In America, I went to SUNY - Cobleskill.

SUNY - Delhi

I'm Yang Ke, from Pengzhou City, Sichuan Province. I am studying in Architecture and Civil Engineering College of Xihua University, majoring in Architectural. From 2008 to 2009, I studied at SUNY - Delhi.

SUNY – Farmingdale State College

Contemplate and grow in experiences.

I'm Wu Ting, from Mianzhu City, Sichuan Province. I study at University of Electronic Science and Technology of China. During my nine months in the US, I went to SUNY – Farmingdale State College, majoring in Computer Science.

I have broadened my vision and have been exposed to more ways of thinking. I will live my life with smile, and embrace my future with confidence.

I'm Liu Huawei, from Shifang City, Sichuan Province. I study Clinical Medicine at Sichuan University. During my nine months in the US, I went to SUNY – Farmingdale State College.

One year experience of studying abroad surpasses reading books for ten years.

I'm Zhang Tingyu, a Qiang Nationality from Beichuan County, Sichuan Province. I study in Management College of Chengdu University of Information Technology, majoring in Engineering Management. In August 2008, I participated at CSC-SUNY 150 program and studied in America for nine month. I studied at SUNY – Farmingdale State College, and my major there was Computer Programming and Information Systems.

Enjoy your everyday life.

I'm Yang Xin, a sophomore from Chengdu University of Information Technology, my major is Communication Engineering. My hometown is Dujiangyan City, which is a cultural heritage of the world. My hometown suffered a lot from the Wenchuan Earthquake, but the people in my hometown stood up with the help from all over the world. In my perspective, my hometown will be better in the future. Being a part of China 150 means a lot to me. I went to Farmingdale State College, and my major was Computer Programming and Information System. In USA, I learned not only the knowledge of my major, but also the world. As a student from the disaster area, I have the responsibility to rebuild my hometown.

One-year experience in America has broadened my views. I really hope that I could become a bridge between China and America for friendly exchanges.

I'm Yang Huihui, from Jiangyou City, Sichuan Province. I study Optoelectronic Engineering and Optical Communication at University of Electronic Science and Technology of China. In America, I studied at SUNY – Farmingdale State College.

I'm Jiang Linglong, from Deyang City, Sichuan Province. I study Automation at Southwest Jiaotong University. In America, I studied at SUNY – Farmingdale State College.

When I sit back and consider the significant events in my past, the important aspects of my current life, and my future goals, the underlying theme is commitment.

I'm Yang Xi, from Wenchuan County, Sichuan Province. I study at School of Economics of Sichuan University, majoring in Finance. In America, I studied Applied Economics at SUNY − Farmingdale State College. I love peace, have passion for almost everything. I believe that I grew up, emotionally, socially, and intellectually, during the year in the United States, and I learnt to smile to challenges. I believe that I am ready to be on my way.

I'm He Wen, from Dujiangyan City, Sichuan Province. I study in the School of Chemistry and Life Science, Leshan Normal University. I went to SUNY − Farmingdale State College from 2008 to 2009.

Sowing seeds of love and sympathy on either side of my life path, I feel my pain eased and tears dried by the fragrance of blossoming along the long journey. With love, I have everything.

I'm Zhang Mian, from Mianzhu City, Sichuan Province. I study at School of Management and Economy in Southwest Petroleum University, majoring in Business Administration. From 2008 to 2009, I studied at School of Business in SUNY − Farmingdale State College, majoring in Business Administration.

Pursue knowledge assiduously; perfect self endlessly.

I'm Yang Jin, from Lushan County, Sichuan Province. I study at Southwest Jiaotong University. In America I went to SUNY – Farmingdale State College.

I found fraternity had no national boundaries. It is everywhere.

I'm Li Chun'e, from Pengzhou City, Sichuan Province. I study Construction Management at Southwest Petroleum University. In America, I studied Construction Management at SUNY – Farmingdale State College.

Dreams are soft, yet they can hold up faiths as firm as rocks.

I'm Zhong Hao, from University of Electronic Science and Technology of China, majoring in Software Engineering. In America, I studied at SUNY – Farmingdale State College.

SUNY – Genesee Community College

I'm Li Yikun, from Mianyang City, Sichuan Province. I study Engineering Mechanics at Sichuan University. During my nine months in the US, I went to SUNY – Genesee Community College, majoring in Engineering Science.

"A thousand mile trip begins with first step."

I'm Yu Haiyi, from Chongzhou City, Sichuan Province. I study Electronic and Information Engineering at Southwest University of Science and Technology. I studied at SUNY – Genesee Community College when I was in the USA. I have many hobbies, for example, ball games, swimming and reading.

I'm Feng Yeting, from Dujiangyan City, Sichuan Province. I study at Leshan Normal University. During my nine months in the US, I went to SUNY – Genesee Community College.

Travelling a thousand miles is better than reading a thousand volumes of books. My trip to America has benefited me a lot.

I'm Tan Tian, from Deyang City, Sichuan Province. I study Communication Engineering at University of Electronic Science and Technology of China. In America, I studied at SUNY – Genesee Community College. I'm fond of sports and traveling. And my dream is to travel to every country around the world.

Life with diversity is a colorful life!

I'm Peng Changrui, from Jiangyou City, Sichuan Province. I study Electrical Engineering and Information at Sichuan University. In America, I studied at SUNY – Genesee Community College. I'm an easy-going and optimistic person. I like making friends and sharing all the happiness with my friends and family. I always try to do everything well and always keep going, and never give up! I have a dream and try to make it come true. I'm still working hard for my beautiful future!

By studying in the US for one year, I found myself more mature and confident. I start to have my own view about everything. I feel really glad that I can be the cultural bridge between China and the US. I tried something to make Americans know more about China, and now I'm busy with making Chinese know more about the US. I hope the friendship between China and the US lasts forever!

Herkimer County Community College

As a group of lucky kids after the disaster, we are growing with endless gratitude and lofty ambition.

I'm Chen Xiaoxi, from Mianyang City, Sichuan Province. I study English at Sichuan Normal University. During my nine months in the US, I went to Herkimer County Community College.

I've learned the value of respect, gratitude and compromise during the past year in America, so whenever I think of the wonderful time there, I can't help smiling.

I'm Yao Tong, from Mianyang City, Sichuan Province. I study Insurance at Southwestern University of Finance and Economics. From 2008 to 2009, I studied at Herkimer County Community College. This past year seems to be a wonderful dream to me. I tried my best to live everyday to the fullest. I love nature, next to it, art, so I enjoyed going hiking on the trail and staring at all kinds of paintings in art gallery. The world was open to me when I communicated with people of totally different backgrounds. Many interesting courses and international friends gave me access to all kinds of information. Gradually I have learned to respect other people, be grateful and I have come to know the importance of compromise. Seeing, thinking and travelling make me the person I am. I firmly believe that my life will be more meaningful only if I try my best to make my hometown a better place. I will keep going and keep pursuing my dream because I have no time to waste.

Despite all frustrations and difficulties in the last nine months, I was happy.

I'm Chen Liangke, from Dujiangyan City, Sichuan Province. I study English at University of Electronic Science and Technology of China. I studied at Herkimer County Community College from 2008 to 2009, majoring in General Study.

I'm Huang Qinghua, from Guangyuan City, Sichuan Province. I study at Leshan Normal University. During my nine months in the US, I went to Herkimer County Community College.

I will pursue my dream with all my heart, never being too proud for gaining or immensely depressed for loss.

I'm Mi Na, from Deyang City, Sichuan Province. I am an English major student from School of Foreign Language for Economics and Trade, Southwestern University of Finance and Economics. In America, I studied at Herkimer County Community College. This great studying experience in the USA has made my life more colorful, and has also helped me grow up. I learnt not only exceptional knowledge, but also something important about life, experiencing a special "baptism" on my soul.

I'm Pu Wei, from Deyang City, Sichuan Province. I study Finance at Southwestern University of Finance and Economics. In America, I went to Herkimer County Community College. In May 2008, I worked as a volunteer after the Wenchuan Earthquake.

I really appreciate this life-changing expreience!

I'm Li Shiyue, from Santai County, Mianyang City. I study at Southwestern University of Finance and Economics. My major is Bilingual Finance. From 2008 to 2009, I studied at Herkimer County Community College.

The most valuable part I got in US is the progress of thinking.

I'm Pu Heling, from Pingwu County, Sichuan Province. I study English at University of Electronic Science and Technology of China. In America, I studied at Herkimer County Community College.

SUNY – Jamestown Community College

After nine months in the US, I have learned how to be independent, how to have self-respect, and how to be strong. I experienced the beauty of a superpower and the beauty of a foreign country. My sophomore year is special and perfect.

I'm Du Pengfei, from Mianyang City, Sichuan Province. I'm from Sichuan University, and my major is Mechanical Design, Manufacturing and Automation. In America, I studied at SUNY – Jamestown Community College. "Being intelligent, noble" is the credo of my life. It is my honor to be a member of CSC-SUNY 150 Program, and to have success in this one-year transfer!

I'm Qin Yuxin, from Mianzhu City, Sichuan Province. I study at Sichuan Normal University. In America, I studied at SUNY – Jamestown Community College.

Sometimes it is experiencing that really matters.
This time, I experienced and gained.

I'm Yang Yongyi, from Dujiangyan City, Sichuan Province. I study at University of Electronic Science and Technology of China. In America, I studied at SUNY − Jamestown Community College.

The future will be more wonderful because we have experienced that special one year.

I'm Yi Qingying, from Pengzhou City, Sichuan Province. I study at University of Electronic Science and Technology of China. In America, I studied at SUNY − Jamestown Community College. I like talking with people because I can tell them my feelings and know their feelings as well; I like sports because I can feel the full energy of life; I like travelling because I can experience a quite different world from what I have; I like the world because it is full of love and hope.

SUNY − Monroe Community College

I'm Xie Yue, from Shifang City, Sichuan Province. I study Teaching Chinese as a Second Language at Sichuan Normal University. During my nine months in the US, I went to Monroe Community College.

I'm Zhou Chenchen, from Dujiangyan City, Sichuan Province. I study at Leshan Normal University. During my nine months in the US, I went to Monroe Community College.

SUNY – Maritime College

Life is like a box of chocolates. You never know what you are gonna get.

I'm Li Chengxi, from Dujiangyan City, Sichuan Province. I study Oil and Gas Storage and Transportation at Southwest Petroleum University. From 2008 to 2009, I studied at SUNY – Maritime College.

Every opportunity is to be grasped; every hope is to be cherished.

I'm He Shiming, from Shifang City, Sichuan Province. I study at Sichuan Agricultural University, majoring in International Economics and Trade. I was a committee member of Student Body, Deputy Director of Part-Time Job Students Union, Vice Director of English Association. From 2008 to 2009, I studied at SUNY – Maritime College.

My name is Lu Shanshan, from Mianzhu City, Sichuan Province. I study International Business and Trade at China West Normal University. In America, I studied at SUNY – Maritime College. What impressed me most is that our professors were so close to the students, and cared about our studies. We respect each other mutually.

SUNY – Oswego

If you try, nothing is impossible!

I'm Xie Jian, from Mianyang City, Sichuan Province. I study Financial Management at Xihua University. In America, I studied at SUNY – Oswego.

To have your own interest is very fabulous, to find your own interest and make it as your own business of your whole life is the most fabulous thing in the world.

I'm Xu Jian, from Jiangyou City, Sichuan Province. I study English at Sichuan Agricultural University. In America, I studied at SUNY – Oswego.

SUNY – Plattsburgh

Dreams and the fighting for the dreams make youth meaningful!

I'm Wang Yali, from Mianzhu City, Sichuan Province. I study English in Foreign Language Department of China West Normal University. My hobbies are Chinese traditional calligraphy, music and studying foreign languages. In America, I studied English Language and Literature at SUNY – Plattsburgh.

I'm Dai Xiaoli, from Pengzhou City, Sichuan Province. I study Finance at Southwest Jiaotong University. During my nine months in the US, I went to SUNY－Plattsburgh, majoring in Finance.

Make every minute counts!

My name is Tang Xuewen, a junior studying in 2006 ACCA(Association of Chartered Certified Accountants) Program, Business School of Sichuan University. My hometown Deyang, a picturesque city located at the southwest of China, is famous as a heavy machinery manufacturing base as well as the earthquake happened in May, 2008. With the financial assistance from the government and the help and support from people around the country and the world, all the reconstruction goes on well. Being out-going and optimistic, I am keen on gaining new experience and trying new things. This type of personality helps me easily get adapted to the new environment of living and studying in the US. The nine months I spent in SUNY－Plattsburgh during which I learned a lot and became more and more mature and independent would be precious memory and wealth for the rest of my life.

I always believe "no pains, no gains."

I'm Wu Dan, from Deyang City, Sichuan Province. I study Logistics Engineering at Southwest Jiaotong University. In America, I went to SUNY－Plattsburgh.

SUNY – Potsdam

The outside world is really awesome; I want to live my own life!

I'm Wang Ju, from Deyang City, Sichuan Province. I study English Education at China West Normal University. In America, I studied English Language and Literature at SUNY – Potsdam.

I'm Wang Bo, from Mianyang City, Sichuan Province. I study Law at Sichuan Normal University. During my nine months in the US, I went to SUNY – Potsdam.

I'm Zhang Yuqin, from Mianzhu City, Sichuan Province. I study Business English at Xihua University. In America, I studied at SUNY – Potsdam.

Stony Brook University

Discard the dregs and take the essence. By learning others' merits, we correct our faults.

I'm Wei Xiaofen, from Mianyang City, Sichuan Province. I study Electrical Engineering and Automation at Southwest Jiaotong University. I got a chance to study in America for nine months after the disastrous earthquake in my hometown Sichuan. During the two semesters, I have learned a lot and have broadened my view, which I will put to use what I have learned to help with the reconstruction of my hometown.